Praise for *Stop Checking Your Likes*

"One part reality check, one part gut check ...
Stop Checking Your Likes is a rally cry to stop seeking external validation, start leveraging the best parts of yourself (yes, we all have
'em) and embrace life on your terms."

— **Jonathan Fields,** founder of Good Life Project® and
creator of the Sparketypes®

"Susie Moore is a breath of fresh air in the world of entrepreneurship. She's an amazing example of what you can do when you live
an apology-free life. Her new book comes at the perfect time and
will be a game changer."

— **Denise Duffield-Thomas,** author of *Chillpreneur*

"Susie Moore's energy, enthusiasm, and hustle are unmatched. If you
want to take something all the way in your life — without apologizing for a second — she'll show you how!"

— **Fran Hauser,** author of *The Myth of the Nice Girl*

"Susie Moore continues to deliver wit, sass, and no-nonsense insights.
I always come away from her work both amused and educated."

— **Brad Yates,** Emotional Freedom Technique expert

"If Susie Moore is telling you how to live an approval-free life, run,
don't walk! She is the mentor that every woman needs, from budding thought leaders to seasoned entrepreneurs."

— **Julie Solomon,** speaker and host of the
award-winning *The Influencer* podcast

"Ever since I met Susie Moore, I can't stop talking about her. But instead of telling me to shut up about Susie, everyone thanks me for
pointing them to her. When you meet the happiest, most confident,
most action-taking person you've ever encountered, you want to

know everything they're doing and then copy shamelessly. So you'll find me here, doing whatever Susie says and does. She's changed the way I live my life."

— **Laura Belgray,** award-winning copywriter
and cocreator of the Copy Cure

"There's *no* person better to show you how to become confident than Susie Moore. She's the real deal. No matter your background or beliefs or how low your self-esteem, if you're willing to trust her, she'll show you just how self-assured and authentically yourself you can really be."

— **Ruth Soukup,** *New York Times* bestselling author of
Living Well, Spending Less

"Susie Moore is a powerhouse — highly energetic, positive, generous, and creative."

— **Bruce Littlefield,** *New York Times* bestselling author

"Susie Moore is the rare type of human who transforms every room she walks into; her confidence and exuberance are palpable. But Susie doesn't stop at being the life of any party — she's also an incredible life coach who has effortlessly guided me through challenging life experiences. She always seems to know the most loving, wise, and empowering thing to say to help me move past any personal issue. There's no way you won't feel more confident and joyful just by being in her presence. I can't think of a single better person to teach people about confidence than Susie Moore. Don't hesitate to learn from her — it will change your life for the better."

— **Melyssa Griffin,** entrepreneur and host of
Pursuit with Purpose

"Readers can't get enough of Susie Moore's positivity, energy, and drive. She's doing the things so many of us dream of — building an empire while mastering the plucky Instagram story — and making it look not only easy but fun."

— **Libby Kane,** deputy editor of *Business Insider*

"If I could keep Susie Moore in my back pocket at all times, I would! Her sharp, savvy, cheerful, and simple guidance is unparalleled and genuinely helps people of all ages, races, and backgrounds take charge of their success. Working with Susie has helped me take bold action without waiting on permission or approval from anyone else! I can't recommend her or her writing enough. Gobble up her words and let them fuel your big dreams and mission! Susie Moore is the real deal!"

— **Jamie Jensen,** award-winning screenwriter and host of the *Creatives Making Money* podcast

"Susie Moore is a giant lighthouse that shows us how to let life be easy and have fun in this wild journey. She has incredible wisdom to offer, and her genuine, girl-next-door lovability makes her the perfect person to have as a mentor and a cheerleader by your side."

— **Cathy Heller,** host of the *Don't Keep Your Day Job* podcast

"Susie Moore is one of those people who lights you up the moment you meet her. She is one of the most dedicated people I know when it comes to personal development and unapologetically going after what you want. If you want to learn from a woman who has gone against the odds to create a truly admirable business and life, Susie is your woman."

— **Sunny Lenarduzzi,** entrepreneur

"A valuable book for anyone seeking greater joy and freedom in this age of distraction and social media comparison."

— **Robin Sharma,** bestselling author of *The Monk Who Sold His Ferrari* and *The 5AM Club*

"Susie Moore has a truly special gift of making you feel like you can do absolutely *anything* your heart desires — and actually showing you how to achieve it. Her book is highly practical, relatable, and fun."

— **Farnoosh Torabi,** host of *So Money*
and bestselling author of *When She Makes More*

"Most people feel like they need permission to succeed. But as Susie Moore points out, that's just not true. *Stop Checking Your Likes* helps us shed our dependence on other people's approval."

— **Michael Hyatt,** *New York Times* bestselling author of
Your Best Year Ever

"Susie Moore's work shows us that passion is the key ingredient to financial success. She'll help you identify it, cultivate it, and put it to work to make you rich in every sense of the word. In an increasingly merit-based gig economy, Susie's fusion of personal and professional coaching is the competitive advantage every aspiring entrepreneur needs."

— **Adam Auriemma,** editor in chief of *Money* magazine

STOP CHECKING YOUR LIKES

STOP 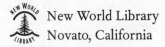 CHECKING YOUR LIKES

Shake Off the Need for Approval and Live an Incredible Life

SUSIE MOORE

New World Library
Novato, California

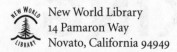 New World Library
14 Pamaron Way
Novato, California 94949

Text design by Tona Pearce Myers

Library of Congress Cataloging-in-Publication data is available.

First printing, April 2020
ISBN 978-1-60868-673-5
Ebook ISBN 978-1-60868-674-2

Printed in Canada on 100% postconsumer-waste recycled paper

 New World Library is proud to be a Gold Certified Environmentally Responsible Publisher. Publisher certification awarded by Green Press Initiative.

10   9   8   7   6   5   4   3   2

*To my beautiful, unique, wise, complicated,
rebel parents (one in this world, one in the next).
Thank you for encouraging my rebel spirit, too.*

Contents

Broken Dreams

On my first wedding day, I was nineteen years old. And at that tender age, I'd already faced some of life's biggest challenges: being on welfare as a kid, growing up in women's shelters, surviving an abusive, alcoholic, drug-addicted father, caring for a depressed and unstable mother, moving across the world with nothing but a few hundred dollars in the bank. It's safe to say that I knew more than most people about all the ways life can go wrong. But on the day of my wedding, I couldn't think about the rest of my life going in any direction other than "perfectly right."

Can you relate to that happy, hopeful feeling? That life is finally on track?

I was marrying someone I was madly in love with. If there's one word for what a young, hopeful woman feels on her wedding day, I think it's this: *possibility*. Oh, the dreams! The magic of what's to come! The pure potential of what you'll achieve in your life with love by your side. It's the beginning of the rest of your life, right? #couplegoals

As I drove to the beach where my wedding was about to take place, my soon-to-be mother-in-law sat next to me, telling me how beautiful I looked. The sun was shining in its full Australian force, even though it was a crisp winter morning.

I was flattered, of course, but truly, I *felt* beautiful. My dusty-rose dress was neat and perfect, with tiny pearl buttons working their way up to the collarbone, and my skin was glowing with all the excitement (plus a little fake tanner — I'm English, and it *was* the winter, after all!).

As the view of the seashore whipped past us, the seagulls diving and soaring overhead, I remember her saying that although we were young, some people get marriage right early on, while other people never do — even after many marriages. That felt true. And I felt certain about what was coming next. Certainty is one of the best feelings, isn't it?

Emotions were running high that morning: the nerves and joy and excitement, and that undefinable emotion that just sticks in your stomach when you know something important is happening. It feels like the day belongs exclusively to you. The world bows to you. Everyone celebrates with you. And I would go so far as to say that other people are never happier or more enthusiastic about your life than they are when your wedding day approaches.

That day, I felt like *this was it*. After all the challenges I'd faced, life was finally going to be easy. Everything would be simpler from here on out. Because I'd made a smart choice in marrying the man whom my heart told me to. Right?

And then.

And then, *when it doesn't work out*, when you realize how incompatible you are together, you're incredibly sad. Second-guessing your judgment leaves you feeling desperate and aimless. And worse still, *everyone who wished you well is saddened*, and you feel guilty about it. It feels like it's your fault. It's as if another little crack in the world appears, just more proof that life goes wrong. It's impossible to make it better for everyone involved. And when you want the people around you to be impressed and happy with you but you feel like you're letting them down instead, well, that just feels miserable.

Do you know that sinking feeling of having to let people down? Worrying about what they'll all think? Sick to let them see you fail at something? The failure can be anything — a marriage, a business, a health goal. It happens to us all.

But here's the truth: we don't have to be strong or perfect all the time. We're allowed to be scared, we're allowed to fail, and yes, *we're allowed to let people down*. And we don't need their constant approval. If you're being honest with yourself, you know that some bad things have already happened in your life, and they will continue to happen. If you're alive on this earth for any amount of time, there *will* be suffering. You'll feel sad. You'll feel scared. Life is full of uncertainty and change, and at times, pain, depression, and darkness.

The good news is, we can comfort ourselves — and this book is full of strategies that lead to contentment, even when things don't go the way you want them to. But ultimately, the only way to lasting happiness is to live your life as an imperfect but first-rate version of yourself. It's far too easy to forget that. To make allowances for others or to be influenced by their approval. Losing the real you is the least conspicuous yet easiest thing to do in the world. Because the world makes it so easy.

The Lunacy of Likes

Just so ya know up front, this isn't *really* a book about social media, so why am I talking about "likes," friend?

Because they've become the current measurement (and public representation) of external approval. Of fitting in. Of how good we're allowed to feel. And frankly, this is proof that the world's gone mad.

We spend *way* too much time looking for the thumbs-up or red heart that's become the modern measurement of how accepted, wanted, or valued we are. It's absurd. Like, if aliens were watching human beings from another planet and saw them constantly checking a small screen in their hands for an emoji to quantify their self-worth, they'd write us off as lunatics. *And they'd be right.*

Seeking external approval has become so natural that we don't even realize we're doing it — but the cost is huge. The cost is the life you could have if you stepped away for a second and let your inner wisdom (not your smartphone software) be your guide.

But there's also good news: you have an undeletable permission slip within you to be, do, and have whatever you want. No one goes through life without hardship, but you don't need others' approval to know yourself and to make the right choices for you. In fact, learning to wean yourself off that approval is the key to freedom. True success means choosing freedom — freedom from needing others' approval, freedom to pursue who you are and want to become. And it's *almost always* an option. That's what this book will help you see. All the beautiful options before you.

Let me let you in on a little secret as we begin. The person you are today? It's old news. It's a result of decisions and actions made in the past. If you're happy with it — great! If you're not — also great! *Did you know that when you look at the stars at night, it's old light? The light that reaches your vision has traveled over thousands of years.*

It's the same when you look in the mirror. The reflection

you see is a result of what's already been in your life, of what's led you to today. You're here to direct what's next to come *on your terms*, to find out who you are and to hold on to it. And to do it without always worrying about what "they" will say.

This isn't a self-help book. It's a sanity book that'll help you find your way back to yourself if, like most of us, you've forgotten the power you have within. Robin Sharma, author of *The Monk Who Sold His Ferrari*, said, "One of the saddest things in life is to get to the end and look back in regret, knowing that you could have been, done, and had so much more."

The Approval Trap

What more is missing for you? In what ways are you letting yourself get mired in what I like to call the "approval trap," the need for external acceptance of your internal needs and desires? Whatever your "more" is, there's a good chance that the need for approval is keeping you stuck in some way. Maybe you:

Care for someone but your parents won't like his career or religion? Approval trap.

Want a career in the arts but everyone in your family is in law, so you're in law school? Approval trap.

Want to increase your income but think you need higher education to do so? Approval trap.

Desire to wear leg warmers to lunch but are concerned that trendy Tiffany will laugh her face off? Approval trap.

Realize you don't actually want kids but decide you'll probably have two anyway in order "not to be weird." And your mom wants grandkids. Approval trap, squared!

Have wanted to get divorced for the past decade but you're worried about what the neighbors/church/in-laws will think? Approval trap, trap, trap.

And if we've gotten even this far together, I know you're ready to spring loose from those traps. And I'll be here to support you. *Everyone* can use support, especially in making empowering shifts like the ones you're about to make. Because everyone is allowed to be, do, and have whatever they want. It's our birthright. We all just get a little confused along the way.

Declaration of Intent

So can we get into an agreement together?

Let's sign a declaration right here, right now. (Grab a pen — I'll wait!)

Our mutual declaration of intent is this:

I'm going to give it all I've got, and you're going to give me all you've got.

Here are the ways I'm giving it all I've got:

In writing this book, I'll speak the absolute, unvarnished truth and won't hold back at all (even though I'll admit it: reliving some of these memories that I've revisited over the course of writing this book was painful, and they *still* make me want to run and hide).

I'll share with you the real tools and techniques that I use to achieve success and that I have successfully introduced to countless life-coaching clients. I've tried a ton of different variations on a ton of different themes over the course of my career, and I can tell you in all honesty that *these are the ones that work.*

But I can only do so much, dear reader.

And here's how you need to give it all you've got. Your intent in reading this can be one thing: to take complete responsibility for your daily freedom, joy, and success.

To open yourself to becoming more self-directed and more

self-approving — and to remain constantly curious about the process.

Are you with me? I hope so. Because the longer we hesitate, the longer it takes for those gorgeous desires we have for our lives to show up. So if you're in this with me, freedom-from-approval-seeker, sign on the dotted line!

Signed by ....

Print name ....

Date ....

Now that you're on board, I've got a few starter tips. Read this book at your own pace. If you want to laugh, cry a bit, or even put me down for a while, please do. I'll dust myself off. (In this book you'll learn how easy it is not to take things personally!)

Remember — this life thing is supposed to be fun. So let's go at it big-time, shall we?

Oh, and a final request, if you please. Put your phone away while you read on. Your likes can wait. Your freedom can't.

As you complete each chapter, you may notice your shoulders relaxing and a feeling of lightness expanding. Creative ideas might flow rapidly. You might feel more loving and accepting of others. Mini pings of euphoria are normal. This means you're on the right course. It means you're giving it all you've got...and you've got this.

Yours in love,
Susie
XO

CHAPTER ONE

Your Parents Effed You Up...
Go for It Anyway

They fuck you up, your mum and dad.
They may not mean to, but they do.
They fill you with the faults they had.
And add some extra, just for you.

PHILIP LARKIN, "This Be the Verse"

My sister is named after my dad's mistress. He demanded it and my mom was too tired and depressed to fight him on it.

"That's a pretty name!" she hears a lot.

"Thanks. I'm named after a family friend," she answers.

I mean, it's not a lie. Lovers are friends, too, right?

We were born into a love triangle. My dad was in love with Rita, a wealthy Polish woman, who was married and had no intention of leaving or divorcing her husband. To keep my dad "occupied" while she was with her husband, she would procure and manage girlfriends for him. She'd then swiftly cut them off if she felt like she had lost control when he appeared to develop a genuine interest in them. She even booked and paid for an abortion for one girlfriend.

She introduced my (also Polish) mom to my dad. My mom didn't have money and wasn't glamorous and so wasn't considered threatening.

Both times my mom was pregnant — once with my sister and once with me — my dad's "best friend" Rita insisted that she get abortions. My mom refused. And so, here we are. Here I am.

There are many strange things about my childhood, but I don't think I've heard of this happening before, in any other family. Whenever I confide in someone about it, the response is a pretty unanimously, "What the??!!"

Yep.

This response has shown up in my life a fair amount, in fact. You'll read lots of peculiar stories in this book, and there's just one reason why I feel confident telling them: if you think any human, or family, is "normal," you simply don't know them well enough.

It's not their fault, but every parent has messed up their kid(s) in some way. We forget that our parents are just humans who were kids like us once, too. And they certainly aren't perfect. They have a lot of their own approval seeking going on within them, too. And hey, they had parents, too. And their parents had parents. It didn't start with them. If you think you may have escaped this, think for a second how a parent's praise and validation can really lift you up. And how being reprimanded or rejected by a parent can fill you with unease and shame. We care what they think. They shape how we feel about ourselves and the world. And it's very easy to think this isn't even happening.

In my coaching sessions — and in life — I avoid asking, "So

what's wrong with this person?" The real question we wanna ask is, "*What's happened to this person?*"

As adults, we're constantly projecting the environment we were put into, the things that happened to us, and the beliefs we inherited during our most formative years.

It all starts early, my friend.

This isn't to hate on our parents. They're just doing their best — we all are. This fact cannot be overstated. And the truth is, even the least praiseworthy parent can bestow great gifts on their kids. We treasure those and enjoy them throughout our life. This is true of my family, too.

Parental Lessons

My mom was born in war-torn Nazi-Soviet occupied Poland in 1942, into complete poverty. She grew up fighting for whatever rations of bread, potatoes, and water her family could find. She remembers most clearly the daily hunger and bitter cold in the winter, made worse by the lack of warm clothes and shoes. And it wasn't until she was in her early twenties that she managed to flee to England.

In England she had a failed marriage to a Mauritian man, with whom she had three daughters (my three eldest sisters), and another failed relationship with my father (who never married her and had violent, unpredictable outbursts and multiple other women), with whom she had two daughters. Her life experiences have shaped in her the following beliefs that she projects:

- Hardship is necessary.
- Rich people can be very miserable (and evil).
- Don't trust others too readily because it's shocking what people can be capable of, even those closest to you.

She's never felt truly worthy of many of the good things that we all deserve as human beings. But she was essentially a single mom of five girls, so I learned independence, resilience, and inner strength from her. I also learned how to move from country to country with ease (so far, I've lived in five). My mom also taught me never to be jealous of another person. To love people who love me. To never cling to a man. To take a chance. To love reading autobiographies. To save. To relax more. To be kind. To always look for a bargain. To not be ashamed of my poor and unstable upbringing. To not worry about pleasing everyone. To not be afraid to ask. To enjoy simple pleasures (the bird! the trees! the raindrops on the leaves!).

My late dad was a complicated person. He was paradoxically incredibly smart and loving yet completely scary and abusive at times. It was like he was two totally unrelated people. In his youth he had knee surgery for an injury he sustained from playing rugby and became addicted to painkillers, which turned into a full-blown drug and alcohol addiction (he actually kept ecstasy pills in his socks). Back then there was no talk of an opioid epidemic that leads to lifetime addiction. His struggle followed him to the end, when he died at age fifty-nine from heart failure.

My mom left him for the first time when I was six months old because she wouldn't give him our last ten pounds for a bottle of Smirnoff. We needed the cash for the electricity meter (back then, people used to feed the meter with coins to pay their utility bill). He was so desperate for booze that he lit a lighter and held it to my head, threatening to burn me if she didn't give it to him. It was her first walk-out moment (even after a black eye and a nearly broken jaw, it took a threat to her child for a change to happen — maternal love is fierce).

That's how addicted he was and how wild he could act (she still remembers how crazy his eyes looked, and she physically recoils when describing them more than three decades later). It wasn't the first time she'd leave, a pattern many people in abusive, dysfunctional relationships are familiar with. My mom still maintains that her ability to be quiet and calm and not provoke him possibly saved her life. I can't help but concur. In a rage, my dad once threw a barstool at me. Dumbfounded, I threw it back. Luckily for us both, we had terrible throwing skills.

And yet, after he survived a heart attack in his fifties, my mom encouraged my relationship with my father, and we moved closer to him after years of keeping a distance and living in shelters to avoid him. She'd been to Al-Anon a lot by then, and we all grew to understand that addiction is an illness, not a choice. The older and sicker he got, the meeker he became. And I got to know my dad as a human being before he died, when I was nineteen. I saw his tender and sensitive sides. This taught me not to judge anyone too quickly when only seeing one version of them. Jekyll and Hyde are real, folks (anyone who loves an addict I'm sure will be feeling me here — to this day no other person has ever evoked such a range of emotions within me).

And so, my dad also taught me a deep love of literature. And to bring joy and lightness through surprises. He'd put candy under our pillows, and one day he wore a balaclava to the gas station and said "jellybeans, please," as he proceeded to *pay* for them. The gas station attendant went white in the face. My sister and I died laughing. He'd send letters disputing a speeding ticket with "Season's Greetings!" and "Get Well Soon!" stickers on the envelope. Not to mention the time he sent a copy of a local history book he authored to Buckingham Palace. The royal family always sends a courtesy thank-you letter for all the gifts they receive, and he photocopied the response, liquid-papered over their text, and wrote "her majesty is enjoying the book, and keeps it at her bedside." (He kept this framed above his desk, of course, and showed every single visitor to the house, including the religious mission workers, who soon regretted knocking.)

My dad showed me that you must always help a friend in need, something his Jewish mother instilled in him strongly (one time during a sober stretch a sick neighbor asked to borrow money, and my dad gave him more than he asked for and insisted it was his gift, something I've always remembered). He taught me how to laugh at the ordinary, small things. How to be sarcastic. How to have fun in daily rebellion (you don't need to pay the parking meter if you just stop for ten minutes, and if you're shopping in the supermarket, the chips you snack on while cruising the aisles are complimentary). How to parallel park. How to win at Scrabble. How to cook a roast lamb and really enjoy it. How humor trumps everything else, and how it can ameliorate almost any pain.

Looking at the Bad Stuff

But what about the rest of the stuff we learn from our parents? The bad stuff that holds us back a lot of the time? We can investigate it a little, right? Question it? Be curious about it?

We're allowed to do that and *still love the people who raised us. Part of us does, whether we like it or not. Children love who they need to love.*

Recently, I was having a coffee with a well-known stylist in New York, and she told me that a lot of the fashion rules we inherit as women come from our mothers. Beliefs like "never wear a red coat!" or "jeans with holes in them are for tramps" or "your handbag must always match your shoes!"

And this stuff — however outdated or irrelevant now — *stays with us.* Now, a red coat may or may not be your style, but that's not the point. The point is that we're always listening to and learning from other people. We have to in the beginning, just to survive. But our lives don't stop there. We have the ultimate say in what we become, have, and even wear in our adulthood.

Fashion wasn't my mom's thing at all. I offloaded on my poor stylist friend all about it when she was probably expecting a light chat about fall trends. I explained to her that when I was growing up, clothing was a touchy subject in my household because you had to have money to be selective, right? My family lived on donations from local families, hand-me-downs from neighbors, and clothing from the school donation baskets.

I remember the desperate ache for approval I felt as a kid wearing used clothes. But my mom's indifference to what we all wore remained ironclad: "It's clean, has no wrinkles, so why are you complaining?"

It was humiliating for me. I lived in fear of being caught wearing a friend's cast-off item that they might recognize. I would spend hours thinking of how I could change a small detail — even a single button — to keep people from suspecting it was the same garment.

Even when it was hot one day in the classroom, I refused to take off a layer, despite sweating at my desk after running around outside. Why? In case "cool Rosie" saw I was in her cardigan (it had her name written on the inside in permanent marker: ROSIE KIM). I mean, if I had been caught in her hand-me-down cardie, what would Rosie think? What would everyone else think? That I'm poor? That I'm not good enough to have my own clothes? That I'm beneath them or even… invisible?

Pleasing the "They"

As a kid, you desperately want approval and will do anything to get it. And it's understandable in a kid, right? Because you just want to blend in. Standing out even in the smallest way can feel risky.

But what might feel true in an elementary-school classroom is absolutely, completely not true in the real world. Just try to think of even one huge success story you know about a person who completely blended in or who staunchly followed the rules and never went their own way. Go ahead, rack your brains: there isn't one. The people we read about and look up to are never the ones who lead their lives consumed by the need for others' approval. They're self-directed, not in a prison of pleasing. This includes, in many cases, being comfortable detaching with love from their parents' expectations and desires for them.

Somewhere along the line, these stand-out people learned something very true and very important: that they themselves are their own best asset. They learned that they're special and that nourishing that specialness means they should avoid listening to the voice of the collective "they" as much as possible. You know the "they" I'm referring to: the people we constantly talk about who tell us how to "live life right" — a college degree, a spouse, a close family, macrobiotic muffins for the kids (who are above average at school, of course). This internalized voice of the "they" tells us we need to be like everyone else if we want to be normal and worthy.

But we act that way to please the "they" a lot of the time, don't we? We want everyone to like us, to accept us. We just want to fit in and gain approval — and we'll go to crazy lengths to do so. We spend money we don't have going to destination weddings for people we don't like that much, we dedicate our lives to careers that don't excite us because they sound impressive, and we laugh at jokes we secretly think are stupid, even offensive.

Maybe your parents did that, too. Maybe they still do it. But it's not going to make you happy. It's not going to help you to know yourself. How do I know this?

Because I had to get over seeking the approval of others early on. There's no way a kid like me, who lived in homeless shelters with a nomadic, depressed mother and an addicted father, fit the ideals of the regular families on TV — with their own houses (gardens, even!), no daily screaming, and no police showing up at the door at night because the neighbors reported drug use or suspected domestic violence (what fun!).

I had every reason to be ashamed of my unusual family. And I was. So what can you do when you're stuck in an environment that feels wrong to you? You can minimize how much your circumstances really affect you. You control what you can. You can choose to be quiet and tune in to yourself. (I mean, what other sane choice is there?) And it turns out that even as a kid, you have more power than you think. When we give our survival instincts a chance, they're stronger than our shame.

This instinct divinely led me to start on a self-help journey when I was fifteen, when I found *The Magic of Thinking Big* by David Schwartz in a bookstore for 50 pence (63 cents). It opened my eyes to the world of choice and the power we all have as individuals. Everything changed for me that day. I haven't stopped reading since (one of the most popular articles I ever wrote is called "Top 5 Lessons from 500+ Self-Help Books" — Google it for the CliffsNotes version of this book!).

And as my young adult life was taking its own inner shape, I fantasized about things I wanted to do when I was an adult:

- Live in New York City
- Have a big job that paid me a ton of money (so I could take care of my mom if she needed it)
- Write for fancy magazines
- Be in a "normal" marriage with a man who respected me and loved me fiercely
- Do important work that made other people feel happier
- Be the fairy princess of a unicorn ranch

And the truth is, I achieved these goals simply because I tapped into the inner, real, powerful me I came to understand existed. I had to. I loved my parents but did not want a life like theirs. I learned that to create a different kind of life, you must *do things differently*.

DIRECT MESSAGE

Simple, right? If you want a different result, you have to do things *differently*. Where might you already notice yourself repeating something not useful or healthy right now — even a small family pattern you might recognize in yourself? It can be dangerously quiet!

In some ways, I was lucky to have had the childhood I had, because I got started on this path of self-discovery before many people get to. In fact, I got to tick off all these childhood goals by the time I turned thirty. (Except, sadly, for the unicorn ranch. That ambition is still unreached.) But it doesn't matter when you start — what's important is that you get started. You can make this shift at any time. You can pursue your goals and passions with the belief that you deserve for them to become real-life manifestations.

After living in women's shelters as a kid, I learned how parents are just like us. They're scared, too — just taller and older. And the power they have to make choices as grown-ups can scare them a lot because every choice brings a consequence. When I was six or seven years old, a woman I lived with in the shelter told me that her husband used to put pebbles in the driveway so he'd know if she left the house. She stayed for years, enduring all sorts of behavior control and abuse. Her parents (and in-laws) were Catholic, and divorce didn't feel like an option. She thought she *had* to stay, since they were wealthy and respected churchgoers. And so I learned early on that "staying in your lane" and not ruffling feathers isn't just exhausting but dangerous, too.

This is why I'm obsessed with overcoming this approval-seeking problem: *because I had every reason to live a small, scared life.* I had an unstable upbringing, I was shuttled around to more than twenty schools, my family was riddled with addiction and mental illness, I received no formal education after the age of eighteen, and I was divorced when I was twenty-three. But along the way, I've realized that the mark of success isn't *escaping* life's challenges and the suffering. Because suffering is a given, no matter who you are or what you have. It's about working through the challenges and facing the suffering, knowing you have options. And that you'll be okay.

> **DIRECT MESSAGE**
>
> Never underestimate the fact that you have options in almost every situation. No matter how hopeless something seems, there are always at least three solutions to every problem (more on this to come). The more options you allow yourself to see, the more empowered you'll always be. That even rhymes.

We're so used to falling for approval traps — big and small — that we don't even know how much we're holding back sometimes. But I know one thing for sure: provided that your intentions are good, you need *zero* permission in this world to do whatever you want. There's no such thing as a good excuse. Because it's still a dang excuse. You're born with that permission slip we talked about in the introduction. You just lost it somewhere along the way on a day you probably don't even remember. And I get why you dropped it. It can be really scary out there. And plenty of people will tell you what you can and cannot be, do, and have.

It's okay even if your mom and dad were those people. They did their best for you. But now that you're an adult, it's time for you to do the best for yourself.

Check this:

❑ Take some time to consider what beliefs you inherited. Most people never do this — they just accept family beliefs as fact.

❑ Question what beliefs might not be useful anymore. Allow yourself space to replace them with what feels right for you. Your heart knows.

❑ Lovingly accept that your parents had their lives but that this is your time. They forged their path and made their choices; the baton's now in your paws.

❑ Forgive your parents. They're human, just like you.

❑ Get excited about the unlimited possibilities of *your* life! Just think about them. A million options are available to you right now. Have you ever considered that? And if you want to, buy a red coat and wear it with ripped jeans.

CHAPTER TWO

No One Else Knows What They're Doing, Either

Life, wrote a friend of mine, is a public performance
on the violin, in which you must learn
the instrument as you go along.

E. M. FORSTER, *A Room with a View*

My friends joke that I'm the least-qualified person they know. I'm not originally from the United States, I didn't graduate from college, and I certainly didn't have any family "connections," unless you count my dad's well-known drug dealer "Lips" (everyone called him that because he had big lips). But I was able to do most of what I've wanted in my career because of just one thing I learned: *everything you need to succeed is already within you.*

When I was twenty-five, my now husband, Heath, and I moved to New York City. It was 2009, the job market was bad, and I needed a job, fast. Heath had one that paid him barely enough to cover our living expenses, so our credit card debt was on the up while our savings were going down. Often, whenever friends or family would check in to see how the job search was going, I couldn't help but feel there was an undercurrent of "Gosh, I really hope you're not screwed."

I'd pound the pavement every single day, trying to get interviews, meetings, coffees with whoever would say yes. I was reaching out to second-, third-, and four-hundredth-degree connections on LinkedIn. My life was a string of meetings, coffees, more meetings, and phone calls. This process went on for what seemed like forever (in retrospect, it was really about three months). In that time, I received zero job offers. Nada!

Starting to feel a little deflated, on one particularly freezing day, I had coffee with a new person I'd been introduced to, Donnovan, a super connected media entrepreneur who knew the industry landscape. We met at an iconic NYC restaurant, Balthazar. At the end of the coffee/interview he said, "Look, I don't have a job for you, but you're gonna be just fine! I'll see who else I know that's looking to hire."

It was a relief. His vote of approval was much appreciated. It meant I could relax for a second. But in reflecting on that moment now, I realize I didn't really need it. A couple of weeks later, my persistence paid off: I received an offer from a tech start-up to do a job that I didn't really know how to do. I didn't care. I knew I'd be able to learn the ropes quickly, and I was happy to finally be making some money.

Winning at Politics

Fast-forward a few years, and I was at a new tech start-up, doing a new job that I was also "unqualified" for. My position involved getting video advertising dollars from big companies and helping them initiate advertising campaigns through our proprietary technology, which allowed them to run video ads online (yes, like those short video ads that interrupt your You-Tube viewing time. Don't hate me!).

In 2012 one of the cofounders of the start-up I worked for called me out of the blue about an opportunity. He asked if I was interested in working in DC for the remainder of the year to see if I could generate some political advertising money to put on our platform. To this day, I am not sure why he asked me, but I like to think that he saw me as someone who got results and was open to new projects.

It was the Romney-Obama race, and it was *extra* harsh. The clients all joked, "New York is descending on DC for the dollars, and then we won't see them for four more years." That city is seriously cutthroat. And I was a brand-new-to-the-place *foreigner,* no less.

This was unlike anything I had ever done. As a native Brit, I had absolutely no understanding of the US political system. Zip. Zero. Zilch. All I knew at that point was that Obama was running again — I wasn't even sure who the Republican candidate was! So to give myself a crash course in US politics, I watched CNN, MSNBC, and FOX like an addict and read hours of *Politico* to get myself up to speed and grasp who was who and what the heck what going on.

Then, between June and November, I spent the majority of my time in DC selling video advertising campaigns to political activation committees and advertising agencies. My new title was political sales director, and my second home became the W Hotel opposite the White House. The local taxi drivers even started to recognize me. "Back to the W?" one asked, as I dashed into his car, my ear glued to my phone. I was surprised he knew my destination, but his recognition helped me feel a ping of joy — they were getting to know me here!

I worked that unique, difficult-to-penetrate, and highly complex market like my life depended on it. One night I even had two steak dinners back to back — one at 6:30 and another at 9:00 — to accommodate two different client schedules.

My boss said he would be "thrilled" if I generated $500,000 in advertising. But by November 3, 2012, when the last voting polls closed on the West Coast, I'd generated almost $3,000,000. What's the moral of this story? I should carve out my niche as a political expert? No. I had found my calling in Washington? Certainly not.

DIRECT MESSAGE

The moral of this story is this: you can do hard things when the word *no* means nothing ("no thing!") to you, and when you don't wait for permission to succeed at something. And that you can totally succeed when you have to learn as you go.

I had no clue about anything political. I didn't know the difference between Congress and the Senate (shh...I still kinda don't). And DC media buyers were obsessed with "voter file data" and specific "swing-state high-female-ratio targets" so, naturally, I didn't have a clue what they were talking about. I had to understand how it all worked, fast. But the truth is, I got the basics down, and that was enough. In fact, I consistently find that the basics are *more* than enough in a lot of cases. If you're an unshakable optimist and forge ahead undisappointed by rejection, then look out, world!

I know this sounds overly simple, but that's the magic of

it — it *really is* that simple. Think about it. Aren't the best and most wonderful things in life pretty (deceptively sometimes, even) simple? We make it all harder than it has to be. My goal was to book $500,000 in ad revenue, and I left come November with *nearly $3,000,000*. I credit this huge win to focusing on what I did have: a strong work ethic, a healthy tolerance for rejection (more on that to come later!), and a ton of optimism. This was opposed to focusing on what I didn't have: any connections in DC, an understanding of US politics, or a bachelor's degree in government (or in anything for that matter). I wasn't even a US citizen who could vote. This was my first time in this market. *I had no reason to succeed apart from a belief that I could.* And I understood that not knowing what to do doesn't have to stop you from doing it anyway.

Reaching, and even surpassing, my goal (and earning a big bonus as well — another lesson learned: *always* ask for what feels fair) showed me what you can do in a short amount of time with massive application and belief. And get this: the biggest deal I closed was due to an off-chance tip from a new connection I'd made.

It came in the form of a last-minute meeting, on my way back to New York, with a small firm I hadn't heard of before. I almost didn't make it because I was worried I'd miss my train. But for some reason, I felt called to go. This wasn't one of the meetings I had worked so hard to secure; it came my way easily. I felt it was a little universal back pat and blessing, a reward for my dedication. When you get busy, the universe — much of the time unpredictably but with more fervor than you can imagine — meets you halfway and overdelivers. I've heard endless stories like this. Those with a bias toward action win. But this I know for sure: so often, we don't give the universe the opportunity to meet us on the road. We give up too soon. We think that other people know what they're doing and that we don't — and that's a lie. No one knows. Success and failure are on the same road; success is just further down that road. And the road has no finish line. But did you find a cozy bench to rest on a few miles in somewhere, kicking off your shoes and enjoying a mini Pringles pack? To people-watch instead of powering on? It's okay. We've all done it. The road doesn't disappear. Your sneakers have endless mileage in them. You can slip 'em back on in a second. There'll be plenty of Pringles in your future, too. And from an even prettier vantage point.

The fact is that no one can give you any power. You're already powerful. You just need to recognize it and claim it like an enthusiastic bingo winner: "Me, me! Over here, over here!" I felt that way when I went on to become the resident life coach at one of the biggest millennial-focused health and wellness websites in the world without any formal coaching certification. I also felt that way as one of the top salespeople in my advertising career, despite not being a "techy" person or even college educated like some of my Ivy League peers (I'd just smile and nod when techy terms were thrown around in meetings).

DIRECT MESSAGE

If there's one word that'll help you live a more successful, joyful, rich life in which you're naturally magnetic to opportunity, it's not *hustle*, *strive*, *focus*, *persevere*, or even *believe*. It's *relax*. Stop worrying so much. Realize how many options lie before you. And then — go for yours! Because as English comedian Ricky Gervais said, "No one else knows what they're doing, either." Winners are just willing to not know and still go!

Yes, even perfectly put-together Rachel with her master's degree in behavioral marketing and her knowledge of every obscure term in the field doesn't have it "figured out." Even though she's always at the office ten minutes early, has a super smart answer for everything, and *seems* like she has an extra ten years of experience in the field, I promise you, she doesn't actually know what she's doing, either. Because *no one does.*

We're constantly overestimating other people and their level of competence because we can't see what's going on in their minds, and we often really overestimate the value of formal education and "credentials" more than resourcefulness, practical knowledge, and the courage to just go for it. We can't see how little a certificate or even an advanced degree really prepares (or doesn't prepare) someone for the difficulties of real-world application. Frankly, because only *we* see our deepest fears, we think life's easier for other people. Their fears and insecurities are invisible to us. But they exist. They make mistakes, too (funny how the mistakes don't show up on Facebook or Instagram).

Impostor Syndrome

Impostor syndrome is what we experience when we feel we don't deserve our accomplishments, and it happens to basically everybody who stretches outside their comfort zone. We feel like we've fooled others into thinking we're capable and therefore attribute our achievements to blind luck or good timing. Our inability to accept our gifts means we end up feeling like a fraud or an impostor — and on our worst days, we even feel like we're waiting to be exposed.

When I was a kid back in England, visiting one of my friends in a "nice, normal" house, I'd feel like an impostor. Like, if they saw where I lived and what my family was like, they probably wouldn't want to be friends anymore. Among the "nice, normal" people, I'd feel a bit like a wind-up doll: Smile! Be cheerful! Say the right things and never forget to be over-the-top with the thank-yous! *Don't screw it up with these nice people!*

Impostor syndrome not only prevents us from enjoying our lives and success, it also massively limits our potential. When someone feels like a fake, they often find themselves turning down wonderful new opportunities and creative ideas. Or sabotaging the success they've already had. It's the killer of many what-might-have-beens. And it's especially common among high-achieving women. I'm not entirely sure why that is, but I think it's because men don't question themselves as much and women are simply socialized to think smaller. As the poet John Greenleaf Whittier said, "For all sad words of tongue and pen, the saddest are these: 'It might have been.'"

I mean, can we be open for a sec to acknowledging this universal self-sabotaging cover-up we're all a part of? It's hilarious, in a macabre kinda way. We're so obsessed with telling ourselves that other people have it all together, and pretending to have it all together ourselves, when in reality, *nobody has it all together*.

Still not certain? Let's test it! Think of someone who seems to have it all. Maybe people like Martha Stewart, Oprah Winfrey, and Michelle Obama come to mind.

Well.

Martha Stewart went to jail for insider trading. Oprah's openly struggled with her weight for decades. Michelle Obama felt shame over her miscarriages for years, thinking she was the only one. *Celebrities — they're just like us!*

There's even some evidence that Winston Churchill's whole illustrious career was really just an effort to try to please his mother, Jennie, an American socialite. She was fairly neglectful of him when he was a child and adolescent but very approving of and heavily involved in his political career. He loved his mother but could only admire her from a distance, "like a northern star," he once wrote. Churchill was also very disappointed about not being able to please his father enough. And he was prime minister of the United Kingdom from 1940 to 1945, when he led Britain to victory in the Second World War, and again from 1951 to 1955.

Hero Inventory

I dare you to research someone famous you look up to. Go a little deeper than a Wikipedia page — biographies are amazing for this — and I guarantee you'll find stumbles, lack of confidence, failures, and despair peppering their path. If not, sue me.

Write down your hero's name, and then discover what their flaws are. List it out in a journal so that it looks like this:

HERO: _____

_____

_____

_____

FLAWS: _____

_____

_____

_____

_____

Say Yes to Opportunity

Next time an opportunity arises but you question your ability to meet it, what do you say? You say yes. Think Jim Carrey in *Yes Man*. Then learn as you go. On the job! That's how you succeed, by saying yes to life and learning as you go. That's what we're all doing. Because no one is born with a life directory. We're just thrown into the void and left there. Like, "There ya go — now, remember you need to pay rent and taxes!"

If you have dreams and big ambitions, know this: other people are out there going for theirs. They might be less talented than you, less qualified, less many things. But they're saying yes to life and getting on with it. They're achieving *your* goals simply because they're willing to go for it, even though they don't know everything. They know that they're in good company with every other *just-figuring-it-out-along-the-way* human being. They decide to believe in themselves, and that makes all the difference.

Embrace Uncertainty

Even people with unfailing conviction don't know what they're doing for sure *because there are no guarantees in this world*. They don't know what the outcome of their actions will be, but that just doesn't stop them. That's all. They're more courageous amid the uncertainty of it all. And what in life is certain, exactly?

Remember that story I told you in the introduction about the morning of my first wedding, speeding to the ceremony with my mother-in-law, feeling certain and right about everything?

Yeah. There's an old saying that only death and taxes are certain. And honestly, that might just be true. The fact is, you might not even live until the end of today. I know it may seem a bit morbid, but let's face it: dying today is a legit possibility. So what makes you think you can control or truly know anything else, if you can't even guarantee that you'll see another sunrise?

We need to learn how to be okay with not knowing 100 percent that what we're doing is "correct." There are multiple ways to do any one thing, and there are far fewer mistakes than we fear. But feeling clueless and scared are among the most common experiences on earth. Think about it for a moment — isn't that true?

I once coached a NASA employee who was scared to seek a relationship because she thought, "Other women are so natural and confident — how do they know how to be like that? I'm so awkward. I can't date."

The CEO of a marketing firm I worked with called me right before he would be speaking at a thousand-person conference and said, "The last speaker was so good. I want to fake food poisoning right now. I don't know a thing about leadership!" At that point, he had seventeen years in leadership and was an expert on the subject.

Once, the editor in chief of a large, influential magazine told me, "I feel like they give me so much responsibility, not knowing my heart beats so fast every time my boss calls my cell. I always think I'm gonna get fired because I don't really know what I'm doing."

Here's the thing: none of us *ever* really knows what we're doing. So can you relax and enjoy the not-knowing a little more? Because it's all there is and ever will be. The world isn't simply divided into people who know what they're doing and people who don't. There are just *people who do* despite the fear of getting it wrong and *people who don't do* because they're scared to screw up.

You're never alone in the not-knowingness of your decisions and actions. My coworker called me crying during her pregnancy because she was worried that bringing a child into an imperfect world was a selfish thing to do. But as a married thirty-five-year-old woman without kids, I've been told that *not having kids* is selfish. Nobody knows a damn thing. We don't even know, *for sure*, what happens when we die. So can we enjoy ourselves anyway? No other choice is really sane when you stop and think about it.

Life presents challenges and a bucketful of unknown uncertainties to all of us. So learning how to handle what we don't know, and just chilling out a bit, is a big step toward living a self-approved, self-directed life.

Inner Alerts

What if being happy were simpler than we thought? Cracking the code of a life well lived? Deepak Chopra said that our heart is a "cosmic computer." In other words, everything you need to guide and direct you is already within.

One of my first coaching clients, Melissa, said to me, "Susie, when I'm at work as an insurance agent, all I do (secretly) is pin fashion looks together and research vintage jewelry." Her passion was so obvious. She created lookbooks on the weekends, followed designers on Instagram, and always looked beautifully chic, on a pretty tight budget. She just needed to step back to realize it. To acknowledge what she wanted, and then to let it in.

And now, years later? The last I heard was that Melissa's a full-time stylist, navigating her way in the entrepreneurial world. It's not perfect or easy, but she knows it's the right path for her, and she's following it.

Melissa knew what felt right when she was restless at work.

Restlessness can feel annoying in the moment, but if we let it be, it's really a gift — it's like your wisest self telling you, "Nice one on getting us here, but let's keep moving!" And that initial inner alert for Melissa was enough. It got her started. Those inner alerts are always available, on demand. Your computer never shuts down or gets a virus by itself. The only threat to it is your neglect of it. Or sticking your snout into other people's computers.

We have this amazing, wise, eternal intelligence available to us at all times...but what do we do instead of checking in with ourselves? We check our likes! We check our little hearts and thumbs-ups. And when we're busy checking our metaphorical (and literal) likes, we're in a constant needy zone. We're waiting for external support and approval — and we might get it a lot of the time. But then what?

We need it again, and fast, and we become dependent on external validation. When the real deal is actually there in the mirror the whole time. Because only you know the real you. Does anyone else know what you want in your custom salad, where you want to live, who you want to marry, and when? No.

So giving other people so much power and influence over our lives doesn't make any damn sense! *You are your best and only real approval, filtration, and support system. And that's enough.* When you look in the mirror one day and see an elderly face looking back at you, whose eyes do you see? Yours. Whose heartbeat is still keeping you there? Yours. Who do you answer to for all your choices until your final day on earth? Yep — you.

Did you know that the "right" thing for you just has to *feel good to you*? This isn't a narcissistic approach to life — it's actually a generous one. It doesn't mean you should go out and have an affair, rob a bank, or indulge in a gossip session that feels bonding in the moment. All these actions might feel fun for a bit, yes. But they're not loving actions...and so do they actually feel good in the long run?

In the Upanishads, the sacred Indian scriptures, it states: "The good is one thing; the pleasant is another. These two, differing in their ends, both prompt to action. Blessed are they that choose the good; they that choose the pleasant miss the goal" (Katha Upanishad 1:2:1).

Feeling good about something is a *lasting* feeling, and one that might not feel easy at the time. Perhaps the long-term answer that will make you feel good is to do something really, really hard, like break up with someone. Or leave a job you hate. Or decide to move because you feel called to a place. There'll be a mix of other emotions, but one thing will trump it all: the choice will feel right to you. Think: When in the past have you made a good, lasting decision? How did the *rightness* of it feel, even if the process of making it was hard? It was probably a decision that propelled you forward, brought you freedom and expansion, opened you up to more, and didn't hurt anyone else (intentionally).

When something is right, you know it. And that feeling... think about it. How could *anyone else* possibly know it (or feel it) for you? They can't. And before I hear you cry that "doing you" is selfish, know this: the best thing you can do for others is to live at your fullest potential, because we all need real-life role models. If you're living half a life — or you're busy constantly changing parts of who you are to keep those likes steady — do you think that makes you generous, giving, and accepting of others? Heck, no! It makes you prone to judgment, jealousy, and criticism because what we do to others is a reflection of what we do to ourselves. If we don't let ourselves *be* ourselves fully, we'll never support other people being *themselves* fully. There are no exceptions to this.

Clearing Inner Pollution

I have a friend, Catherine, who went to therapy with her husband, James, because he was ready to leave her. She was putting a lot of pressure on him to earn more and think bigger in his career. Catherine's nitpicking and judgment had swelled to a point where her husband would do anything to have some peace. It led them to the therapist's office, where Catherine uncovered that she pressured her husband so much because, coming from an extremely achievement-driven, hardworking family, she always did the same to herself. Failure, or "coasting," was not considered acceptable. She was a high-achieving woman (she worked at Google), and she never let herself off the hook for any mistake. Her husband's easygoing ways offended her long-held — and ultimately, unhealthy — belief that you can't be content without constant perfection and relentless hustle. And when she realized this through professional help, she backed off.

Eckhart Tolle says, "As within, so without: If humans clear inner pollution, then they will also cease to create outer pollution." In the case of Catherine and her husband, the problem wasn't *his* paycheck. It was *her* fixed thinking.

When you have the polluted belief that other people and their approval create your steadiness, you'll always be sitting in a rocky boat. Because there's nothing more unpredictable (and often irrational) than other people's thoughts. Like Catherine seeing James through her high-intensity filter, everyone sees the world and the people in it through their unique filters. For instance, a pageant mom who had been a pageant kid herself might have a filter that makes her see her children's value as being tied to their physical beauty. A musician might prioritize self-expression over structure. It's dizzying to think of trying to peer through more than one filter at a time, and ultimately, we can only see the world through our own.

Not long after her breakthrough in therapy, Catherine said to me, "Accepting James where he is...well...it just feels good." It felt right to her because she loves him and wants to be with him. She doesn't want to pressure him, but the belief system she had before getting help made her think she had to. So that's how you know: You don't consult your parents. Or the best friend you might have outgrown. Or filters out there on a million phone and computer screens. You consult your inner cosmic computer (a good coach or therapist can help you fine-tune it when needed, for sure). Your own inner guide is really the only reliable intelligence there is. *And it knows the next right move for you.*

DIRECT MESSAGE

No one knows everything. No one can 100 percent accurately predict the future — even the next twenty-four hours of it. We're all just doing our best, and when we base our actions on our inner intelligence, we are far more likely to be satisfied with our decisions in the long and short term. Because you're not a plastic bag, drifting through the turbulent winds of other people's approval, powerless. You're an adult with decisions to make about how you're going to spend your life.

The calm confidence you appear to have when you just "do you" in your own quiet way, in the corner of the world that you touch, is sexy as heck, too. People flock to people who seem to know exactly what they're doing, simply because they follow their inner guidance. Being relaxed makes you popular. The irony, eh?

Check this:

- ❏ Recall five times you did something for the first time that was scary. What happened? That's all a courageous life really is. A string of first times.
- ❏ Know that there is no rule book for life. We're all just doing our best based on what we know. Repeat this to yourself anytime you see someone who seems to have everything perfectly together and you are triggered by it. Remind yourself that you don't see the whole picture.
- ❏ Pay attention to impostor syndrome when it pops up (it does for everyone). Say to yourself soothingly, "It's okay — we're becoming X (a speaker, a VP, a good negotiator)!"
- ❏ Remember that the only constants in this world are uncertainty and change. How can anyone know or predict what's coming and how to handle it? They can't. Neither can you. So…relax.
- ❏ If you need help, go get some! Therapy of all kinds has saved many a person (myself included).

CHAPTER THREE

How to Always End Up on Top

*Spending too much time focused on others' strengths
leaves us feeling weak.
Focusing on our own strengths is what,
in fact, makes us strong.*

SIMON SINEK

In childhood, you may have wanted to be Mom's favorite. Or at school, maybe you craved being the teacher's pet. Or maybe you went a different route and got the attention of the "cool kids" by being the class clown. And these days, it's nice when the boss loves you — or when your whole team admires you and thinks *you're* the cool boss, right? And now, as we've talked about, since we're on social media twenty-four-freakin'-seven, we count each and every one of those likes as if they're absolute sustenance. It's like we've come full circle, back to infancy. We're suckling at the teat of our devices! No wonder we're more stressed-out than ever, and no wonder antidepressants are prescribed at least four times more than they were twenty years ago.

While I absolutely recognize that depression is a real medical condition and that mental and emotional health are part of overall health, I also doubt that this massive upswing in antidepressant sales can be *entirely* chalked up to previously undiagnosed mental health issues. I think we're creating a culture that's making us sad.

And it's not our fault. Well, to a point.

I can guarantee you something right now. In some area of your life, you're grossly overestimating *somebody else*. You think this hero of yours has something really special, that they were born with something you weren't blessed with. That they have the Midas touch and that all you can do is watch as they overtake you or keep killing it out there — because hey, *there's the proof*! Right? Look at Instagram pics of them wearing that perfect boho-chic outfit in Lisbon! Or their fancy new job title you just saw via a LinkedIn alert! Or their flawless dinner party conversation (more on that later — I'll even help you dodge questions about family, like I always used to because of my unusual history). And why are they always on the up and up (and how are they always flying first-class, right)?

Here's something to chew on. These things are within you, too. That's why you admire them. They're probably just in hiding. That's why you notice them in someone else in the first place. Think about it:

Are you jealous that a teenage girl sailed solo around the world?

Are you feeling upset that your super meditative friend went on a twenty-one-day silent retreat? (No, thanks)!

Or that she stays on a raw-vegan, macrobiotic, alcohol-free diet for six months at a time? Hmm.

Does it make you feel insecure or behind that another

friend is working every night and all weekend, hardly seeing their kids, to become partner in a top law firm?

I'm going to guess they're on the less-popular end of the envied, I-wish-that-were-me spectrum. Admired, yes. But triggering you? Probably not! If they do trigger you — damn, you're really adventurous.

Ah, but Louise from college with her cool blog and stud boyfriend? That might be another story, right? *Oh, Louise, Louise, Louise. Are those hair extensions? What diet are you doing? How can you be so pretty and funny?* (Her blog is annoyingly entertaining, right? — come on — you read it. And the small spelling mistake you saw on her Instagram post is the only scrap of schadenfreude you're going to get.)

Well, well, well. Of course savvy Louise is going to show a crap-ton of blown-out messy waves pics. And she's going to write a lot. They are *two strengths* that she's got. But who knows what she's lacking? She doesn't have many friends, perhaps? Maybe she's exhausted and her overall health isn't as good as it looks (this is surprisingly common). Perhaps that stud boyfriend has an addictive side or is a philanderer. Maybe the idea of public speaking has her so short of breath, she passed up a maid-of-honor position and disappointed the sister she's always looked up to. Who knows?

The better question is, Who cares?

You.

I know you do. Because I do, too. We all do — to a point. We're human. And we use what's in our environment as reference points. How can we not?

But there's something *much more important* to start caring about right now. And that's what *you've got*. Because when you give what you actually have right this second a little light and thought, you'll find it's so much more than you think. I promise. No matter what we do on this earth, what contribution we make, all of us play an important role, and we usually don't even know it.

For example, it kills me when a woman with kids describes herself as "just a stay-at-home mom." Are you kidding me? I was an au pair for three months in the South of France, and I've never been so exhausted or stretched in my entire life, *ever*. Having a successful corporate job and building a thriving business were a piece of cake compared to looking after kids. You run a house, raise responsible humans, clean up poop, cook, pay the bills, clean up more poop, and do a million other things *without pay* — or frankly, much praise. You can't even take a shower or use the bathroom without bringing the baby in. You're on high alert all day long. You don't get lunch breaks, coffee runs, or paid time off, at least not without thirteen things to pack with you and a dozen planning worries to think about and a bunch of stroller logistics to manage.

Strength Valuation

A friend of mine told me once that it took a divorce lawyer to make her realize how much she's worth. She contributed beyond belief to her marriage: she took a back seat in her career for a bit so her husband could excel and so that her kids could have a parent at home (no judgment here — all parenting is hard, and the choices are personal). But she thought she was worth nothing until a savvy lawyer broke it all down. They were *equals*. I don't care what LinkedIn says.

Picture this. The prices will vary from place to place, but you get the gist:

- Price of a full-time, live-in nanny: $800 a week
- Price of a three-meal-a-day personal chef: $300 a week
- Price of a home manager who shops, organizes, pays bills, takes kids to and from events: $700 a week
- Price of daily housekeeper: $260 a week
- On-call life coach/date/confidant/copilot to spouse: priceless
- Taking a back seat in your career to play support role to your spouse: potentially millions (this is not an overstatement)

> **DIRECT MESSAGE**
>
> This is not about money being a form of validation over anything else (nor is having a job or any particular work that you contribute). It's about not discounting what you're doing, whatever it is. There's so much more value in whatever you're doing right now than you probably believe. What might you be overlooking? Your value as a loyal friend (ahem: therapist/publicist/life coach)? The flowers you planted that make people pause, smell, and smile? The way you listen to your coworker as she thinks through a problem? The intrepid travel you do that inspires others to see more of the world? Appreciating your value, however you're showing up and just being, matters.

As someone who doesn't have a perfect résumé, I know it's the confidence, not just the competence, that counts.

One day I met a mom in my building whose kid was at the

constantly-asking-why stage of his childhood. *Why is that man cleaning the windows? Why do some people have two dogs? Why are the windows black on that car?* I'd bump into them often, and one afternoon we were checking our mail at the same time.

"Why are the mailboxes locked, Mom?" he asked. She explained that important documents are delivered via mail and so we have to keep our letters safe. I said to her something along the lines of, "Hey, ya know what? I hope you don't mind me saying, but you're such a nice mom! You're so thorough and patient with his good questions!"

And guess how she responded?

She cried.

Yep. She told me that no one compliments motherhood. That it's thankless most of the time. "No one tells you you're doing a good job!" she said, looking in her well-stocked bag for a Kleenex.

She then told me she missed her job and the constant good feedback she used to get from coworkers. She was looking forward to getting back to work once her son started school, which he would do in just a few months. I was momentarily flooded with affection for her and said, "I'll help! Let me help! I used to be a recruiter and we can do some interviewing role-play! And I'll tell you how to network your way back in!"

And so we had tea at her place. I asked her about what she used to do, and she told me she was a team secretary at an architectural firm for eleven years. It was a great job, and she was clearly competent, having been there for so long and having risen through the ranks over time. I asked her why she was great at the job.

"Um, well, I was always on time, *even early*, to work."

On time? That's it? Certainly punctuality matters, but an intern on their first day can be on time, *even early*.

"What else?" I asked.

"Hmm. I have a pretty good attitude. I'm happy to stay late to get the job done!"

I had to take a deep breath.

Arriving early and staying late are great employee traits but, *come on!* I was looking for what really made her special.

What else?

> **DIRECT MESSAGE**
>
> Practicing active listening and always asking, "What else?" are great ways to get to the bottom of almost anything.

We sat for almost an hour, and after a significant amount of probing — "what else?" many times over — we got to the nitty-gritty of what made this woman stand out. She is:

- A natural problem solver
- Innovative
- Calm under pressure
- Efficient
- Proficient with a million forms of software

To arrive at this conclusion, I asked her this (and you should steal it for yourself!): "What was some good feedback you received at work? Tell me all the praise you remember."

She'd say things like: "My boss loved how I knew when he was running late. I'd shift around his afternoon schedule and let everyone know what to expect without him asking me first. If it was too tight, I'd have to just make a call and combine meetings or cancel the least pressing one."

Ahhh, *so you anticipate your team's needs in advance!* How wonderful! And helpful. Making calendar calls on the spot like that? That takes some innovative thinking right there!

What else?

"Near a project deadline, it was naturally a high-stress time. I'm pretty calm and people would tell me that I don't freak out like some of the others — stuff like that. Because stress seems contagious."

Yes, yes, yes! Now we're getting somewhere! Calm under pressure! Resilient! Efficient in high-stress environments! What a gem this woman was.

Do you see what we're getting at here?

She had no idea what she had going for her. I had to root it out of her, like a pig searching for truffles. Yes, her software skills could use brushing up, maybe (whose couldn't?), but that was no reason to think that someone else was a more qualified candidate than her.

She had to shine a light on what she had and stop overly revering others who were still in the corporate mix just because a 2.0 download of some unremarkable software was on their laptop. Big. Deal. Think for a second: Where are you overlooking a significant contribution you make — or can make? This doesn't apply just to women, moms, or stay-at-home parents. It applies to all of us.

When Heath and I moved to New York, and I was interviewing all over the place, I had no college degree or American connections to tout. But I knew there were two things I do well: I connect with people easily (largely by asking questions), and I'm also pretty persuasive. But heck, having these qualities didn't wipe out my nerves. I still felt like a scared kid half the time, a child who'd been given way too much to handle. But I knew I had to soothe myself into a confident mindset in order to get the best out of myself. As I sat on the 1 train on my way to a meeting or interview, I'd replay past career situations in my mind. I'd relive them, my chest tight, hoping the people in this impressive, huge city could find me impressive, too.

And when my interviewers asked me about my education (which was clearly absent on my résumé), I didn't lie. But I did deflect the question by asking about *their* education.

It went something like this:

"So, you didn't go to school here, Susie?"

I straightened my shoulders, not wanting to appear discouraged, and said, "I didn't. Where did you go to school? There are so many great universities in America!"

And then I'd listen. That was it. Potential disaster averted. People love talking about themselves, and I knew that.

On the persuasive side, I knew I'd need to gloss over the fact that I had no local experience. Coming from Australia and working with a couple of American clients, I knew that some New York execs wouldn't necessarily place much value on my foreign experience. So I thought about it. I'd worked at a host of cool Australian and Asian companies, but my interviewers wouldn't recognize those. Even though I'd never worked in America, I'd worked with American brands. And so, I *did* have American experience! That made me as good as a local, right? So that is all I talked about. American brands. Expedia, Allrecipes, even LinkedIn. Dot-com or dot-au — who cares? I focused on the dot-com part.

I had two job offers and accepted the highest-paying one (it was $75,000). But five years later by the time I was thirty, I was earning $500K a year in the advertising technology field, as we talked about a little earlier. And I got there just by doing one simple thing: *using what I had*. My ability to connect with people and be persuasive took me a long way. And most of my peers, many of whom had degrees from Ivy League universities and/or MBAs, were making way less than I was — because they were terrible at knowing their strengths.

DIRECT MESSAGE

Whenever it's appropriate for you, just wear a blazer. Blazers make everyone look and feel more impressive. You can get them for $40 at H&M! Zara also makes great ones. This goes for both men and women. You'll also make more money as a blazer-wearing person. It's an unspoken, universal rule.

What strengths are you overlooking because you're too busy noticing how you are at Excel, how you don't have a master's degree, how social graces don't come easily to you, or how short you are compared to your tall, elegant friend?

STOP.

Knowing your strengths is vital. Our time on earth, and our unique talent, is too precious for us to be focusing on what's missing. There's nothing to prove to anyone but ourselves. No one is perfect or has it all going on. The most perfect-seeming among us simply work really well with what they've got.

And no one, *no one*, has every skill under the sun. And everyone, yes, *everyone*, has problems. Author Regina Brett said, "If we all threw our problems in a pile and saw everyone else's, we'd grab ours back."

So if we're going to envy someone's perfect hair and perfect marriage, we also have to envy their behind-the-scenes problems like their credit card debt, anxiety struggles, verbally abusive partner, or eating disorder. But we just don't know what these behind-the-scene issues are — and it's not our business. It bears repeating: as proof, just look around you. Do your best friends post on social media their UTI, their tears over their ex, the rent increase they're freaking out over? Heck, no.

And if it seems that someone doesn't have problems, it means you simply don't know them well enough. Because that's the problem, right? We don't see everybody else's crap. Other people's business is not for our eyes — unless they wish to share it. But we can judge what we *do* see with a more level head. Because it's like a quarter of the full picture in a lot of cases. And what they *do* share? It's the good stuff they've got.

Instead of ruing the strengths of others, you can start putting the spotlight more on your own. This is a really fun thing to do. So few people do it, and it's highly beneficial for those who do. You can even start with something simple like a StrengthsFinder test. Not just knowing but acting on and revealing more of what you've got is life changing. Not to mention that it's a terrible thing to go through life with diamonds in your pocket and be oblivious to them because your attention is on other people's jewels.

Comparing Lunchboxes

When I was a kid, I used to feel jealous of other people's school lunches. Because of my broken home and nomadic family, I went to a lot of schools — more than twenty. We had no money for those cute juice-popper drinks or colorfully packaged Cheez Doodles and sliced apple and carrot packets. At the schools where they didn't give us a free lunch (with a gross, chunky, and far too conspicuous silver token), my packed lunch was always the same. One peanut butter sandwich cut into small squares, and half a banana. My sister would get the other half.

"They have water at school," my mom always said.

I mean, they *did* have water. But lunch was the longest, most exciting part of the whole day. And I certainly had no one to trade snacks with. At lunch I'd eat really fast so no one would see the (lack of) contents in the lunchbox that was too big for my meal. There was a saving grace once — a local church at Christmastime donated lunchboxes to me and my sister. They were the best part about lunch for me. The brand-new pink Barbie lunchbox that went "snap" with a metal buckle.

So if I didn't have the coolest lunch, what did I have?

I had good writing and reading skills.

I nearly always attracted a nice, small group of friends wherever I went.

I had a generally good aptitude for learning most things quickly, despite switching schools a lot.

Do you see something here? As adults, we often compare what's in our metaphorical lunchboxes. We compare our relationship, job status, body type, everything, to that of the person with the best of that one thing. But what percentage of your overall life does any one item in your lunchbox represent, really? It's not the whole picture.

Someone else might have the better-off family, but you're better in the classroom. Someone else might have the newest, trendiest clothes, but you have the oldest, most loyal friends. Another person might have exciting engagement news, but you've just gotten back a perfect health check.

We don't need to compare lunchbox with lunchbox. Or dating life with dating life. Or career with career. It's a skewed, disproportionate measurement, and frankly a lot of the time, if you step back for a second to see it, inaccurate.

And the problem with life and with social media is this: you're just looking at the other person's one-dimensional lunchbox! Yep — it's just one or two things per person a lot of the time! For this person it might be her relationship, for that person, her income. For another, her long legs and cool accent. And it's almost always on the side of what *you do not have*. And even when it does look awesome on the outside (like my cool pink lunchbox, the thought of which still tugs on my heart), what about the inside? Not always so awesome. You just don't know.

Another thing to consider is this. What good might there be in *not having* something you think you really want — at least in this moment?

To continue with the lunchbox example:

- I wasn't a fat kid (those juice boxes and Cheez Doodles looked so appetizing, but they sure don't help childhood obesity rates).
- I always felt compassionate toward other kids who didn't have much. This remains true for me as an adult, and I think it's made me more generous.
- I appreciate *all* nice food now. All of it. More than anything! (Contrast this to Heath, who went to an expensive private school and has a mom who is a brilliant cook, but is a very fussy eater!)

Hey — an unimpressive lunch never killed anyone, either. My mom was certainly never apologetic about what she fed us each day, which oddly helped me and my sister feel better about it.

Sometimes our lack seems so big in our heads that it consumes us. Appreciating our strengths really brings us back to a place of perspective — and relief. I remember one girl at school who was upset because my handwriting was "so much more like the teacher's" than hers. Maybe that was her lunchbox perspective on me! (Hey, looking back, I totally should've traded handwriting lessons for a bag of Ruffles. You live and learn.)

Do you need some critical perspective, too? If you're eyeing what someone else has with a pang, then I'm telling you, you do. Because something serious is happening here. You're not recognizing what's *within you*.

What I've Got

Need help?

Here's how to get over coveting what others have and own what you've got:

- Think: *What am I fixating on in someone else?* Be honest!
- Consider: *How much do I really know about this person?* For example, are they in debt? (So many flashy-looking people are leasing BMWs and living in the red!) Do they struggle with food issues? Is there a fertility challenge in their lives?
- How good is their relationship, truly? Are they and their closest family members all in good health?

Get real about how much you really know about this person. It's probably less than you think. You can make a list like this one.

What I know about Louise:

- Good hair
- Seemingly enviable relationship

What I don't know about Louise:

- If her sex life is at all satisfying
- Whether her mother is nice (or even alive)
- If she regrets not pursuing another career path, even if she's successful in her current role

Now, let's work on positively comparing *you* to other people. It may be uncomfortable at first, but stay at it — nobody is going to see this but you, after all!

Create a list and call it "What I've Got!"

What do you have that a lot of people don't? Caring, healthy parents? Good skin? Quick wit? Let it all out!

Now think of someone you're envious of. How have they actually helped you? Maybe they've unconsciously inspired you to try yoga. Or be more confident at work. Or go for it in traveling to someplace new.

Here's another good one. List all the ways you and this person *are actually similar*. I bet you my Rent the Runway Unlimited membership that this list will be longer than you think. We typically envy people like us because we see ourselves in them — they may just be a tad further along. And that's okay! They were in your shoes once. (We're going to dive into this deeper in chapter 5.)

Try this experiment. Delete all social media apps from your phone, and keep them off for one month. A Yale University course on happiness highlighted that this could actually make you happier than a lump sum of cash. (See? We're all victims of this nonsense.) Yes, really. Delete that app now! I'll wait.

This might sound morbid, but I find it life affirming. That person you overestimate? Well, they're just as likely to be in a car accident or caught in a hurricane as anyone else. Think about that for a second. Don't build them up to be immortal.

They're not. Look at what happened to Princess Diana. In the end, not even all her magnificence and fame or the fact that she was adored worldwide could save her.

Think for a moment. Imagine if Tom Brady wanted to be not just a star quarterback but also a pro tennis player and compete at Wimbledon. Or if Beyoncé wanted to be the world's premier entertainer *and* a prima ballerina. Or if Oprah Winfrey tried to be a fashion designer in addition to being the magnate she is today. What would happen? They'd all be diluted, weaker. They wouldn't be Tom, Beyoncé, and Oprah, the pros of their fields. They know what they've got, and they just continue to work it!

We need all the diverse, unique skills we have in this world. Imagine if we were all doctors. Or handbag designers. Or airplane pilots. Who would save us from fires? Who would bake the bread we eat? Who would be writing the books we read or the songs we love to sing in the shower? Our uniqueness matters. *The only danger is in believing that one person's talent is more valuable than another's.*

Prizing What's Precious

Sometimes, the most important truths are the easiest to overlook. That's why I love *Aesop's Fables* so much. My mom and I would read them to each other at our various kitchen tables when I was a kid, and their wisdom — which has been passed down for 2,500 years! — has always helped the world make sense to me.

I particularly love the story "The Cock and the Jewel," which perfectly illustrates this issue of comparison. I'll retell it here for you.

A cock was once strutting up and down the farmyard among the hens when suddenly he spied something shining amid the straw. "Ho! Ho!" quoth he. "That's for me." And he soon rooted it out from beneath the straw. What did it turn out to be but a pearl that by some chance had been lost in the yard.

"You may be a treasure," quoth Master Cock, "to men that prize you, but for me, I would rather have a single barley-corn than a peck of pearls."

This rooster wanted a piece of corn more than a pearl. What's the moral of the story? Precious things are for those who prize them. So can you prize what you've got and remember that it's precious? This is how you end up on top. Doubling down on your strengths and appreciating them is something that only *you* can do. Our job is to maximize what we have instead of trying to fix or strengthen what we don't. And to keep our peepers off other people's paths. And to treasure our own pearls.

And if you still feel like you come up short (this stuff can take time and practice), then remember this: the best-in-the-world pros typically master one or two things well. Even David, who beat Goliath, was good at only one thing: using a humble slingshot. And we know you've got a lot more than that. So look again. At yourself. Delete those apps and keep them deleted for a bit! And stop sandbagging yourself.

Check this:

❏ Think: *What am I fixating on in someone else?* Then consider: *How much do I really know about this person?*
❏ Create your own "What I've Got!" list, and let it be loooong.
❏ Ask yourself: *Has the person I envy actually helped or subconsciously encouraged me in some way? Could I foster some appreciation instead of angst?*

❏ Delete all social media apps from your phone, and keep them off for one month. And when (if!) you're back online, DM me on Instagram and let me know how it felt! (@susie.moore)

❏ Read over your "What I've Got!" list. What stands out today as something you can really adore? Snap this list and keep it on your phone for regular revisits and safe-keeping. Knowing who you are and what you've got can't help but keep *you* on top.

CHAPTER FOUR

So What?

*Joy is what happens to us when we allow ourselves
to recognize how good things really are.*

MARIANNE WILLIAMSON

One day, I was procrastinating online. It was like any other morning: English breakfast tea by my side, hair in a ponytail, my pup Coco on my lap, a million tabs open. And then — yay! I decided to check out my YouTube channel's comments section. I thought, *"Read the comments," they said. "It'll be fun," they said.* Little did I know.

There it was: one of the meanest comments I've ever seen. There's nothing like seeing a hurtful comment pop up on your screen, completely out of the blue, especially when you're in your sweats, cozied up on your favorite part of your sofa, feeling ready to start the day, thinking pretty good thoughts about the world.

My hurt quickly turned to anger. I was seething. Fuming.

Red-in-the-face mad. I stood up fast (poor, startled Coco leaped to the floor!), and ran to find my phone.

I promptly called my Scottish friend and mentor, Fiona, in a rushed huff, and before she even had a chance to say hello, I charged in: "Guess what? This skanky troll online said I look like a man and that I'm gross!"

Silence.

Was Fiona there?

"Hello?" I asked, uncertain.

"Yeah, Susie. I'm here. So what?" she said, in her distinguished Scottish accent.

So what?

So whaaaattt?

There it was. Two words — and one of the best questions I've ever been asked.

Because, truly, so what?

That took the wind outta my seething sails. I mean, the drama flew out of the convo like air from a popped balloon. Her casual question was so disorienting because it was the best possible response in the world. I had to laugh.

So *what?*

Precisely. I mean, *What's it to me*?

Did this random online comment mean I'm a screw-up? *Nope.* Does it mean I need to give up on life? *Heck, no.* Does it mean I actually look like a man? *Ha!* I've never thought about that, but if someone else thinks it, I guess that's none of my business. And even if it's true, what's wrong with that? We're not put on earth to judge other people's appearances. It's an unkind statement, but it's a reflection of the person criticizing, not the person being criticized.

Applying *So What?*

There's an almost ancient wisdom to this two-word question — *So what?* — and there are a million ways to apply it.

So what? means just *doing you* and not worrying about other people. Everything's okay. Talk about a Buddhist-style, you-can't-really-mess-with-me edge. And so humbly (and concisely!) put.

What are some situations that you can respond to with a *So what?*

- Hearing a rude remark that hurt you?
- Not being included in or invited to something that you *wanted* to be a part of?
- Not being included in or invited to something that you *didn't want* to be a part of (hey, sometimes it still bruises the ego)?
- Not being asked out on a second date?
- Your kid being a bit behind the other kids?
- Being snubbed by a colleague in a meeting when you deserved credit?
- Doing twenty-five instead of your usual forty-five on the elliptical?
- Not getting the job you applied for?
- A friend of your new beau's ignoring you (or making a dumb comment to you) at a party?
- Being out of the cool club at the office?
- Being ghosted by someone you thought had potential?
- Paying a no-show fee for the 7:00 AM workout you skipped for much-needed sleep?

- Not being quite where you thought you'd be at age twenty-eight, thirty-five, sixty?
- Not getting a text back from that flaky friend about weekend plans?
- Screwing up dinner?
- Feeling embarrassed over your family's quirks — like my mom using a tea bag multiple times (because she grew up with nothing so doesn't waste a thing)?
- Being divorced (more on that later!)?
- Feeling guilty about a hangover?
- Having buyer's remorse over something unreturnable?
- Earning less than your best friend (even though you were better at school)?
- Running out of dog food and giving your pup a helping of your mac and cheese instead?
- Not being or having a perfect [fill-in-the-blank]?

So what? contains magic. It means we hold life lightly. And we ultimately come back to remembering what matters most. Magic unfolds when we don't attach pressure, meaning, and weight to things that don't matter as much as we work ourselves up to believe they do. *So what?* brings us back to our natural state of ease and joy.

There's another hidden gem in here, too. When we care less about something "bad happening," other people care less about it, too. The world follows suit. If we make something into a big deal, other people are likely to make it into a big deal as well. We humans are wired for mimicry. Our brains have what are called "mirror neurons," a type of brain cell that responds both when we perform an action and when we witness someone else perform the same action. I learned this when I was an au pair. When a kid fell, I'd laugh and say, "*Aw, lève-toi, Maya! Tu vas bien!* (Get up, Maya! You're okay!)" I'd brush off her knees and smile. She'd look a bit surprised, as if she needed a second to figure out if it were true, and in most cases, she'd be back on her scooter in seconds.

But before I learned to do this, I would look concerned and gasp, "*Oh non! Est-ce que tu vas bien? Montre-moi tes genoux* (Oh no! Are you all right? Show me your knees.)" Scared Maya would cry — and she would not be all right. She'd need hugs, tears wiped from her cheeks, and a *glace à l'eau* (popsicle).

We're so powerful! Do you see that? That stinging comment on YouTube could mean nothing (*So what?*) or could make me Google "plastic surgery to look more feminine."

I chose *So what?*

People tend to mirror us when we're so good at shaking things off because we all secretly want to learn how to do it, too. To be less sensitive. To be more at ease and less flappable. It's a display of strength. And it tires bullies to the point of boredom, so they look elsewhere for a reaction.

You can even find humor in the situation because humor can be the ultimate healer. Heath thought it was particularly hilarious, too, because the comment was partially a reference I didn't get from an *Austin Powers* movie. The anonymous person wrote, "That's a man, baby!"

No One Is Watching

Here's what I've learned — from experience — about failure: *The worst part of "failure" isn't whatever went wrong; it's the worrying what other people will think of you when it does.* When that stranger said something mean about my looks, my first instinct was to delete it so that my friends, peers, even (cough!) *frenemies* wouldn't revel in seeing it. Other people's opinion of what goes wrong in our life often hurts us the most. The thing itself can be endured. We just need to lessen the hold of others' perceptions. Read this paragraph again.

"Failing" is just the undesired result of an action you took. You can live with it. You've done it all your life. Learning to read took time. (You got plenty of pronunciations wrong, right?) So did driving. (I bet you hit a traffic cone or two!) Cooking, too. (If you haven't set off at least two fire alarms, you're not even trying.) It hasn't been all flawless from the beginning, right? But you stayed at it.

But having all those eyes on you when you do it as an adult? When someone dumps you, a business venture goes south, or someone shares an embarrassing story about you? Ouch. So here's what you need to know about that, and pronto: *No one is watching you.*

A few years ago, I was celebrating my thirtieth birthday with a friend, a bottle of champagne, and a lobster roll (the perfect trio!) at Rue 57, a cute NYC restaurant in Midtown. As we were clinking flutes, an older woman — wearing a Chanel jacket and the largest pearl earrings I've ever seen in my life — leaned over the seat and wished me a happy birthday. After I smiled and thanked her, she said, "You know, dear, I tried so hard to be perfect when I was your age. And then I realized no one was watching. Enjoy yourself!" She's right. Because no one is watching you. Everyone is way too busy worrying about themselves.

DIRECT MESSAGE

Worrying that people are watching you is especially common at social events. You might think you said something awkward, but it's forgotten in an instant because other people are thinking, *Is my dress too tight? Do I look pathetic standing here with my phone? What should I do with my hands?* So let go of the pressure to be perfect. Whether you're going to a conference, dinner, work meeting, or party, you don't have to rock the room or dazzle everyone. You can start by just being nice.

Skewed Perceptions

One day I went to Connecticut to have lunch with a friend who'd moved there after having a baby. Another friend was at lunch, too, Renée. I was pleased she'd joined us. Renée was always so impressive to me. She had a big job at JPMorgan in the male-dominated world of Wall Street. She always looked effortlessly elegant. She seemed to have everything she wanted: she was recently married, pregnant, and moving to a nice big house in a wealthy part of Connecticut.

That's why I was so surprised when the words "I feel like a loser" came out of her mouth that day. It seemed so incongruous. She looked incredibly put together as she sipped on a chilled San Pellegrino, rocking a pair of oversize Tiffany sunglasses, skinny jeans, and $700 espadrilles.

"Whaaaaaat?" I asked, confused.

"This place. I feel like a weird suburban loser. I thought it was what I wanted. Now I don't know."

After a few more questions from me (ahem — unsolicited coaching?) she told me she missed city life. She was pretty sure now that Manhattan had been the "cool life" and she was feeling regretful. She had *thought* she wanted the big Connecticut house, with the pool and the PTA meetings and the summers in Nantucket, because it looked so appealing in her friends' Facebook feeds. It seemed like an obvious life goal. And because she felt this settled-down approach was what she *ought* to want. She spent so much time thinking, *We should really move to Connecticut!* and not enough time asking, *Do I even want to move to Connecticut?* She felt homesick for what she had had before.

"Is that true — are you a loser?" I asked.

"Well," she continued, "that's the thing. When I was single in New York City in my midthirties, I felt like a loser. I thought I should be here — doing this mom-life thing. That's what all my married mom friends said. And I wanted it so badly and look, I'm so happy about this kid…"

She continued, confused at her own confusion, looking down. "For some reason I just always feel like a loser. Like, you can't win no matter what you do." She took her sunglasses off and rubbed her forehead. Anyone not privy to the conversation would think this incredibly chic, elegant mama had a headache, not that she was feeling despair over her very nice life. Renée was, by most people's standards, succeeding at everything. But she was getting too caught up in judging herself against what other people — in this case, city corporate types versus stay-at-home-suburban-mom types — were telling her she should want.

Here was a woman who was in a gloriously privileged position. She had a husband she was in love with and a baby on the way and a remarkable career she had built that paid her handsomely. The options for her future were strewn like jewels at her feet. In that moment, if she had truly felt that Manhattan was calling her back, she could have easily returned to her old neighborhood and raised her family there. The city is much safer than it used to be and has some world-class schools. What she was really feeling was just some temporary FOMO (fear of missing out) caused by flicking through a friend's super-fun-looking Insta story about a night of exploring art gallery openings and sipping smoky mezcal cocktails in a trendy new speakeasy in Bushwick. If she had been able to recognize that, hey, she could have smiled at her own memories of her city life, made plans for a weekend stay in the city sometime, and returned to feeling grateful for her beautiful, quiet life in the suburbs.

But despite being successful by every usual measure and smart as a whip, she felt paralyzed. She didn't know what *she* really wanted because she was too concerned with what other people thought was cool. It's easy for us to see that other people's opinions shouldn't matter so much to her. Someone else's paralysis is always more obvious than our own. But that doesn't stop our own emotions from being irrational a lot of the time. That's why we need to employ our brains when processing our emotions and not just to take our initial feelings as facts when they make us feel bad. And not just to succumb to an uncomfortable thought that'll make us suffer — one that might even seep in and own us for a whole day (or longer).

Because people will always find something to criticize, no matter how amazing you are or what you're accomplishing. In fact, I once read in an article written by someone who calls the Dalai Lama a "conman" and states that he "deserves criticism, not adulation." The critic even said, "It is a great insult to the collective intelligence and goodwill of humanity that he is granted the attention that he is." I mean, if the Dalai Lama can be called a conman, what hope is there for the rest of us?

How can we win? We can't. We need the *So what?* to save us. You absolutely cannot win by spending your life pleasing other people. Ever! Do you see that? The only way to win is to be lighter about it all. To *So what?* the damn thing.

Reframing Fear

Fearing what other people think about your perceived failure affects you more than you realize. When you're worried about something going wrong, that concern about other people's perception takes up too much of your attention.

Make a quick list now of five to ten things that went wrong in your life.

Are you still alive? I believe so. If you look back, I mean, *really* look back, you'll probably remember being more scared about what other people would think and say than about the event itself. When I got divorced in my early twenties, despite the pain of it all, in my heart it was a relief. But I was so concerned about other people's judgment. I was wrapped up in worrying that people would make pronouncements like "Young people don't respect marriage" and "She's damaged goods/used up now."

That scared me more than doing life alone.

My friend couldn't afford to take a skiing trip with her old college pals, and get this — she hates skiing! She loathes the cold! "Good!" I said. "Great reason not to go!" But she didn't tell her friends the truth. She made up an excuse about being busy that weekend. "I don't want them to know I don't make as much as they do." She wasn't scared to say no. She was scared to be found out as to why — and what they might think if they knew about her more modest salary.

That's what scared her.

When my client lost a popular employee, he told me, "I can replace her. I already have someone in mind. But I'm worried everyone on the team is going to think I'm a bad leader because she's leaving and I'm her boss. Like, they'll think I can't retain people. Or that my employees don't like me."

That's what scared him.

And when another friend sold seven tickets out of ten to her vision board event, she was secretly pleased to have fewer people in her small living room. "People will fit much better," she said, "but won't people think I'm not that great 'cause I didn't sell it out?"

That's what scared her.

Do you see the pattern here?

The thing itself — whatever life throws our way or whatever decision we make or circumstance we find ourselves in — is almost always okay on its own. But it's the nonsense we pile onto it that screws us up. What if we could let up on ourselves a little? And understand that, just like us, everyone else is concerned with how they're being perceived as well? It's like a psychological disease we all have and don't diagnose.

Let's face it. We all feel like we're failing in some way or another, all the time. But what if the lady in the Chanel jacket was right? That no one is watching? *Exhale!* What a waste all those worried hours have been!

There's tremendous freedom, levity, and joy in allowing

things to be just as they are and in not trying to make them even a wink different to satisfy or impress anyone else. What can you accept as is? What can lose your scornful eye? What can you — dare I say it — accept about yourself and your life? What can you just freakin' enjoy?

> ## DIRECT MESSAGE
>
> If you adopt a *So what?* attitude, everyone will want to know what therapist you're seeing or what inspirational podcast you're listening to. They'll want a bigger slice of you in their world because they'll want your attitude to rub off on them, too, to help ease their sensitivity and anxiety.

Now, be careful how much you ask yourself *So what?* because you might become the most dangerously free person you know.

I get it: your day, circumstances, and life right now probably aren't perfect. But the truth is, they never will be — perfect doesn't exist. But that doesn't mean that imperfection has to kill your vibe. Because *So what?* Not everything needs to be perfect to still be pretty damn good. And remember: no one is watching anyway.

Keeping It Casual

Being more casual (even flippant) about life events that seem pretty serious to some people *does not make you irresponsible*. It makes you a boss. The person who constantly cracks when they hear criticism, weakens when they worry about optics, and is overly sensitive to peer judgment isn't leading the way in anything. They *never* get ahead. They're too trapped. This isn't to be confused with loving, helpful, constructive feedback. And your instinct can pretty much always tell the difference.

I learned to adopt a pretty casual attitude about events that most people find surprising, devastating, or shocking, such as:

- Being the only kid in my family to skip college and go straight to the biz world. (I felt like a baller, at age nineteen, with business cards. *Look, Mom — business cards!*)
- Moving to Australia on my own at age eighteen.
- Taking a job as an au pair in the South of France for a French family, knowing only *bonjour* and *merci*.
- Being married before any of my friends.
- Being divorced before any of my friends.
- Being remarried before any of my friends.
- Leaving a $500K job to go all in on my side hustle.
- Being a ward of the court as a kid.
- Being surrounded by my dad's drug-dealing friends and even his prostitutes (more to come on all that).
- Attending a bunch of different schools as a kid because we moved a lot.

Unusual? Definitely. Life or death? Hell, no. *So what?*

How can you apply this *So what?* attitude to all the nonsense that crops up in your day-to-day life? Here are some examples:

A parent chimes in unkindly on your parenting style.

Say, "Thanks for your insight, Kelly." Smile. Then keep doing you. She's allowed an opinion. *So what?* Let her be happy thinking she's an expert. *What's it to you?*

You skipped a workout and feel guilty as heck.

Remember, there are a million workouts in your future. It's all in your hands. You can work out later today or tomorrow. Set that alarm clock an extra hour early if you want. *So what?*

You're not as close to your BFF anymore.

Time, distance, lifestyle changes, and personal growth separate people. It happens all the time. Stepping off the gas doesn't mean abandoning the car! Being less close is still okay. It's all still love, right?

Or maybe there's been a little issue or a fight. Maybe you can't recover from it. Not every duo is destined for lifelong joined-at-the-hip-ness. Finding that you've become distanced from an old friend is a great opportunity to meet new people and move forward. It doesn't stop you from being grateful for the times you had together. *So what?*

Any relationship ending reminds me of one of my favorite lines from writer Joey Comeau: "You think love has to last forever for it to be real. You think it isn't true love unless it lasts until one of us is dead.... That isn't love. That's dog fighting."

The news is making you crazy.

Is there something you can do — even at the local level — to help? Yep, bad things are always happening in the world, and you'll never be able to control it all. *So what?* Do your bit, what you can, to help others. Consider volunteering with an organization you admire and donating to causes you care about. Doing something feels so much better than just looking at social media and feeling powerless.

Someone offended you with their tactless joke.

Was the joke racist, sexist, or bigoted? If not, then…*so what?*

Your sister is pissed at you for turning down Thanksgiving at her place this year.

There will be more Thanksgivings. She'll get over it in time. And she knows you love her. *So what?*

Someone you know is trying to give the impression they're a huge baller on social media, and you just don't buy their authenticity.

It's not a wrong you need to right. It's a bad use of your time and energy gossiping about how full of nonsense they are. *So what?*

You didn't get the raise you wanted.

Is this a sign that maybe you should look around? Your boss doesn't know what she's losing. You needed the nudge to take action, anyway. It'll only be your salary for a few more months and so…did you guess the answer here? *So. Freakin'. What!*

I heard a funny story once about Albert Einstein. He was, of course, a great scientist, and he was curious about many things …and he also *couldn't fathom why socks get holes so easily*. So one day he gave up socks! Altogether. As simple as that. *So what?* He didn't even wear socks when he was invited for dinner with President Roosevelt. Apparently, he became proud of the fact he didn't wear socks. And as far as we all know, Einstein going sock-free didn't make the sky collapse!

The process of living is difficult for all of us, even the rich and famous. If being rich and famous were the gateway to joy, then celebrities would all be terribly happy and trouble-free, right? But sadly, we see so many beloved famous personalities give way to drug addiction and even suicide.

If you can flip the script, you can even have fun with the drama. Yep, fun. And everyone will want to know how you're attracting so many good new things to you. Because here's an important secret: When we're lighter, our energy skyrockets. It's the law of attraction at its finest. When we're dense and heavy, we just get more of that dense heaviness in our day.

Think — will the divorcée who still talks sh*t about her ex on the daily (and complains to her long-suffering friends every chance she gets) attract a new, compatible beau... or will it be the one who forgives her ex and is having a nice time living her sweet, single life? I'll let you answer that.

And guess what? That perspective works for a lot of things. It's not about ignoring difficult, painful things that happen. It's about applying less meaning to almost *everything* people say about you that bothers you. Because we can't always control what happens to us, but we can control what it means to us. When you realize how unserious this perceived problem is, you allow yourself to realize how good your life really can be. And just like the forgiving divorcée just having fun, who knows what you'll attract?

1. The next time you think people are looking at you in judgment, picture the older woman who came up to me on my birthday and said, "You know, dear, I tried so hard to be perfect when I was your age. And then I realized no one was watching. Enjoy yourself!" And I

want you to drop your shoulders and exhale slowly as you do so. Perspective is everything.

2. Think about an area of your life in which you've been indecisive. Have you been considering a career change or a move? Try clearing away everyone else's influence and think about what *you really want*. Think of Renée, uncertain about whether she wants to be in the suburbs or the city because she's overwhelmed by others' opinions. What would you tell her to do if she were in *your* situation?

3. Right now, identify three people who have bothered you whom you could instead approach with a *So what?* attitude. Have you been hung up on a careless comment about your weight some jerk made? Did someone get under your skin at work? Make a note to remind yourself, the next time you interact with that person, to go into the situation thinking *So what?* in advance.

Check this:

❑ The next time something or someone offends you, play around with a *So what?* response instead. See how good it feels!

❑ Make a list of five to ten things that went wrong in your life. Write down the good things that still happened anyway.

❑ Plan ahead. List a few worries you have about the future. Approach each one with a *So what?* See what happens. Are you still okay? I'll bet you are. Remember, this is about caring less without being careless!

CHAPTER FIVE

Love Yourself, Especially When You Don't "Deserve" It

You are very powerful,
provided you know how powerful you are.

YOGI BHAJAN

I used to work with a guy named Michael when we were both headhunters in Sydney, Australia. He was a funny dude who was *über*confident. Women loved him, and one day he met "the one." He was obsessed with Jenny. She was perfect, he said: tall, blond, big smile, smart as hell, laughed at *all* his jokes. She even forgave him for his chicken-wing addiction. He pretty much became Jenny-obsessed overnight, and we were thrilled for him.

One day, over lunch at the pub, he said to me, "Jenny and I are going to get engaged. I don't know why she wants to marry me, but I'm not gonna convince her otherwise! She's every man's dream." I'd met her at this point, and I can tell you, she was lovely to be around, she clearly adored him, and she was absolutely *hot*. "Even though she's so crazy sometimes, ya know," Michael said. "And she has this weird obsession that she has big legs. She calls herself a pear or an apple or something like that. She's nuts! Her legs are hot as hell."

I told him that all women have their quirks, and he agreed. But over the next few weeks and months, I started hearing less and less about Jenny. He'd cut short any conversations about her, and then one day, I realized Jenny hadn't come up in conversation at all. I asked after her.

Michael said something I've remembered ever since. "Yeah, I dunno about her. Maybe I jumped in too fast. She's great, but I don't know…she also has kinda big legs."

I couldn't believe it. Jenny didn't have big legs. But she convinced Michael she did. More to the point, she had turned him off with her self-criticism. *Why would she do that, repetitively put herself down in front of him?*

For attention? Reassurance? *Compliments?*

Big mistake.

You are your partner's prize. Let them love you! If you need reassurance or someone to tell you the candid truth about whether you ought to improve something physical about yourself, ask an honest friend. Don't ever put yourself down physically. Not once! When I tell *needy-for-reassurance* people Michael's story, they typically stop their self-criticism, pronto.

DIRECT MESSAGE

This isn't about the Michaels of the world. It's about you. It's about you choosing how you talk to and about yourself consciously and intentionally — because you are listening. The way you feel about yourself will dramatically improve. And the world's response to you will follow suit.

Say it with me: *I like my body. I like how I look.* It makes me crazy when I hear people criticize themselves, especially to their partner. It's madness (no one ever hated themselves into anything good). Are you trying to convince the person who loves you that they made a mistake?

Let me repeat: You are your partner's prize! Act like it.

If you can learn to like and value your physical self more, it'll serve you for the rest of your life. The most coveted girl at my high school wasn't the most attractive. She just walked around like she was. Her self-approval rating was unusually high. And the boys responded in kind. We all know someone like that, right? The person who shouldn't be a VP but somehow dominates every boardroom they're in? The average-as-heck Instagrammer with the huge audience?

Louise Hay, in her super popular book *You Can Heal Your Life*, wrote, "You have been criticizing yourself for years, and it hasn't worked. Try approving of yourself and see what happens."

Be Your Own Biggest Fan

As someone who's been a columnist and contributor in the wellness space for years now, I've always found something quite depressing about this subset of online media. Which is, what we're allowed to say about ourselves.

What are we allowed to say about ourselves that's positive? It's like there's an invisible self-approval threshold somewhere and we're not allowed to cross it beyond something along the lines of, "I'm a work in progress." Don't get too big for your booties! Know your place, ya imperfect thing. Tut, tut, tut!

And I say, screw that. I'm sorry, but "I'm a work in progress" just doesn't cut it for me. Not one little bit. I prefer to go a little more Kanye and appreciate who I am with this one life

I've been given. He once said, "Everyone should be their own biggest fan."

I wholeheartedly agree. Can you open up to being your own biggest fan? Or if it feels like too much to go that far this instant, can you at least be on your own side a bit more?

It's so easy to have positive thoughts about the people we love — we think they're talented, funny, clever, special — but have you stopped to consider recently that you just might be those things, too? And that the world sees you that way?

My best friend, Alexis, and I love to relive old memories. Whenever we get together, we marvel at how life goes by, but because we live in different countries (she lives in Australia), we don't see each other as often as we'd like. A year or so ago, however, she came to visit me in New York. One of the days we spent exploring the city, checking out a new MoMA exhibit, and eating from the dim sum carts in Chinatown. That evening, exhausted, we curled up on my couch together, sipped glasses of rosé, and pored through a Target shoebox full of old photos. Looking at each one, we tried to recall what we were thinking and feeling at the time — and had a hilarious, moving hour or two. And then Alexis dug up the *really* old photos (so old they were curling up at the edges). She picked one out and gasped, "Oh man, I looked like *that* when I was twenty-four? I can't believe I thought I was fat!"

"Show me!"

She passed it over, shaking her head at herself, and we looked at the photo together: it was a picture of her and me standing at a bar in Thailand, wearing pretty dresses we had proudly purchased on sale, drinking electric-blue drinks topped with bright red cherries. When I saw it, I thought, *Why was I so self-critical back then? I was cute!*

Try this for yourself. Look back at some old photos, from ten or more years ago. See how good (and young) you look. Now let the past inform the present moment.

You can remember those harsh criticisms you had about yourself a decade ago when you're looking in the mirror *today*. And you can soothe yourself, and let go of current criticisms, in the knowledge that ten years from now, you'll be saying the same thing about how you look today. If not, you'll regret not appreciating the person you are, right now. Precisely as you are.

Here's a great mantra for you: *I've decided to like what I've got.*

For instance, I'm not tall (five-foot-two). I have fine hair. I have fair skin, and I used to go to sunbeds to tan it. I have a curvy — not thin — body type. But this is what I say aloud to myself now:

- I'm perfectly petite! Who'd want to be of average height?
- My friend Joanne spends three hours washing and drying her thick hair — no thanks! I love my quick, easy style.
- I love looking forward to a vacation for an extra reason — to get a nice golden glow.
- (In a bathing suit) This is how the pinup girls looked in the forties — the sexiest era!

What can you turn around, or at least begin to see in a new way?

You can do this with pretty much anything. Deciding to love what you've got is the only sane thing to do, when you think about it. Especially if it's something that you can't or won't change.

Approving of and liking yourself also — surprisingly — makes you easier and more pleasant to be around. Because you're not complaining about yourself and putting pressure on others to pick you up (you may not even realize you're doing this). And criticizing yourself is frankly boring. Because all negativity is boring. But I've never met a person who has described themselves as negative. They're just not aware of how negative they sound and how their energy impacts others. This kind of behavior is insidious. Being negative is so commonplace, too. It's so basic. Whereas if you actually like yourself, you're a shiny light in the world. It makes you unique.

I used to work with a girl named Monique who was a workout fiend and ate very particular food — like Weight Watchers apricot squares — for meals. She'd always say things like, "When I'm not so fat" and "When I lose this muffin top." We would all roll our eyes and the occasional person would jump to defend her, but after a while, we all stopped because we were tired of it. I said to her once, "Monique, you're beautiful. But this nonsense that keeps coming outta your mouth — I'm not going to pay attention anymore, okay? I'm just going to agree with whatever you say."

She complained less, at least to me, after that.

I know it might feel like a stretch, but imagine if instead of obsessing over all the things we don't like about ourselves, we chose to focus on a couple of things that we actually like. Because we create a negative self-image in the mind, and we can destroy it the same way: through focus and repetition.

It's common to reject self-approval until we feel perfect (a moment that obviously never, ever arrives). Can we be okay where we are right now — just a bit more? Or if there's space between where we are and where we would like to be, could that inspire us instead of demotivate us? Great happiness can be had in making progress.

So if you want to get more fit, for example (something I always aspire to), could the current gap between where you are today and where you see yourself next not be so daunting? Could it even be a little bit fun? You get to create fun playlists to walk to! Line up inspirational and entertaining podcasts! Go shopping for some new sneakers! Revel in the fact that for an hour a few times a week no one can bother you because you're in a class without your phone? It can be real *you* time.

Affirmations Work!

I heard a saying once that I often repeat to myself: *Imagine if we obsessed over all the things we love about ourselves.* Can you pick one thing you love (or even just like) about yourself and state it in the mirror right now? Or even with no mirror — just speak the words wherever you are. If it feels uncomfortable, good! Stick with it. Give it a go. Seriously. Notice the subtle shift in how you feel, and enjoy it. It will encourage you to do it some more.

I practice mirror conversation often because of its totally transformational power. You can do it everywhere you go. Look in the mirror when you're taking the elevator, or catch your reflection in the glass as you do some casual window shopping. You can say, "Hello, you clever woman!" or "I love you!" or "Good hair day!" Whatever feels good.

One time I was even busted in a restaurant bathroom. I was loving the gentle mirror lighting, the lush white hand towels, the vanilla smell in there — and I thought, *Girl, you look goooooodddd!*

And I went for it with one of my signature moves — a butt pat and an "I love you, Susie!"

The "I love you" happened *just as a kid walked in on me.* (We've all been there, right? I swear the door was locked!) Of all the things I could've been caught doing in there, she caught me in the act of doing my affirmations. Looking back, I almost wish I'd said: "Do affirmations, not drugs, kid! Lasting happiness!"

Sometime when you're in the privacy of your home, a dressing room, or a nice restaurant bathroom, blow yourself a kiss and pat your butt while doing it! Why not? Have fun with this!

I affirm myself daily. It varies from "You are strong, brave, and special" to "You are wise, hot, and young." Even a simple "You're doing great!" is wonderful. Whatever you need in the moment! Think…what do you need right now?

Yep, there's no shame in the affirmation game. Because affirmations work! And no one even has to know you're doing it. I'll admit the unsuspecting kid looked a little stunned. Caught in the moment, I ended up pretending I had a pain-slash-cramp in my hip and walked out with a totally awkward, apologetic smile!

But in a way, I wish I could sit every kid down (and every adult, too!) and speak about the power of self-approval. It's transformative. It's free. It's available to us all at any moment. If you can choose between affirming and denying yourself, why wouldn't you choose the former? Over and over? What's the sane choice here?

This, of course, applies to far more than the physical. It's about accepting *all* parts of us — our intelligence, our warmth, our cooking skills, our professional experience, our ability to communicate. All of it! One time I gave a talk to large-ish group of people, and a friend met me for a glass of wine afterward at a place close by. When she asked, "How'd it go?" I answered, "Ya know, I think I did well." We said cheers and had a high-vibe girl date over tapas.

Later that week, she texted me: "You know how you said you did a good job at that talk you gave? It made me realize how I never give myself any credit. Like, no credit at all. But I'm going to start doing it!"

It's as if my affirmation of a job well done gave her the freedom and permission to do the same for herself. Where can you be doing this more? Can you acknowledge that you're good at:

- Being a parent?
- Listening to other people?
- Encouraging others?
- Making other people feel comfortable in your presence?
- Taking risks?
- Telling the truth?
- Organizing your closet?
- Researching trips?
- Taking care of your dog?

The list goes on and on! What can you appreciate about yourself?

I did this exercise with a group of women once, and here are some examples of what came up:

- "I love that I am a very loyal friend."
- "I love that I'm an awesome cook."
- "I love that I'm resilient."
- "I love that at age sixty-five I started ballroom dancing."
- "I love that I am a great saver — I have a good nest egg way before I need it."
- "I love that I'm an adoring wife to my husband of twenty-three years."

- "I love that I always wake up in a good mood."
- "I love that I pick up languages easily."
- "I love that I've been sober for fourteen and a half years."
- "I love that I've read so many books."
- "I love that I got out of an abusive marriage."
- "I love that I'm extremely passionate about my work."

Here's the true gift in all this: when you affirm yourself, it unofficially green-lights others to do the same.

I'm told that I'm a good encourager. It's true: I'm enthusiastic about uplifting others. But my secret is, *I encourage myself on the daily first.* I have to. As the old saying goes, you can't give away what you don't have. And the ultimate goal in this world is to spread a little light around to make it all easier for one another, right? To love thy neighbor matters, yes. But remember the second part of that important commandment, too, will you?

The commandment reads "Love thy neighbor as thyself." See? Don't forget *thyself!!!* There cannot be neighborly love without thyself love! Are you starting to see that loving and approving of yourself is therefore a highly generous act?

So can you like what you've got, what you do, and how you do it a little more? Because it's not just about you. Everything you put out there is contagious. It passes on.

Are you struggling to remember who you are and what you've achieved?

Twelve Magic Moments

Here's a coaching exercise I've used for years that I call the Twelve Magic Moments. It can be very helpful when you're having trouble seeing your own awesomeness:

Choose three things you're proud of in relation to your family.
These can be varied — anything from "Helped my mom with
all her groceries after she had minor surgery once" to "Survived my dad's alcoholism." They can come from any time in
your life.

Next, choose three things you're proud of in your work. This
can include your schoolwork as a kid, housework that you do
to make your home beautiful, and/or work that you're proud
of in your career. This can look like a mix of stuff big and small,
old and new, from, "A client loved my presentation last week"
to "I won a Latin award when I was thirteen."

**Now, choose three things you're proud of in your relationships
with friends.** Think of small things and big, from "I stood up to
a domineering friend in a loving way, even though it scared me
at the time" to "I cleaned my friend's house for her and stocked
her freezer with casseroles after her dad died."

**Finally, choose three things you're proud of in your relation-
ship with yourself.** This is my favorite. It can be something as
simple as cooking for yourself regularly, graduating from college, getting a driver's license, moving to a new city, taking a
bold risk…whatever you're most proud of. It does *not* have to
be impressive by anyone else's standards. Just yours.

Remind yourself of all these past achievements. Reflect on each
one for a minute.

Remember how you felt at the time of each achievement.
Were all of these super easy from the get-go? Probably not.
Maybe you didn't feel capable or good enough or ready, but
you did them anyway. What was the outcome of each accom-
plishment? What has it shown you? What can this lead to next?

It's the foundation of all your life's future possibilities. How freaking exciting is that?

I reflect on some of my life successes when I'm feeling down. Our egos have a short memory — they only remember what we've typically failed at over the past week or month. It's important not to discount what you've overcome. And to be able to remind yourself of who you really are *on demand*. When I'm about to do something new and scary in my business, I remind myself that I worked in Washington DC with no experience and started a side hustle that took off. We can do hard things because we've *already* done hard things!

Getting there can take time, I know. This practice requires repetition. And maybe you need to forgive yourself for a few things first.

Here's another great tool for releasing yourself from any shame, regret, or guilt you may be holding. It helps dissolve hurt with the power of self-compassion. And self-compassion is the highest form of self-help. This process is called Loving Little Me.

Loving Little Me

Find a photo of yourself as a kid. Hold it in your hands and look into your own eyes. If you don't have a photo, that's fine; you can just picture yourself as a child.

Take a few deep breaths.

Say "Hi, sweet [your name]."

Close your eyes.

Take a few more deep breaths and then ask the younger you, "What do you have to tell me?"

Listen.

What she or he might say can surprise you.

Keep listening and breathing.

Think of everything little you endured to get you where you are in this moment.

Look at little you. Pause and don't rush this.

Every time you criticize yourself, hurt yourself, dislike yourself, you're criticizing, hurting, disliking little you. Does she or he deserve it?

No way.

Say "[your name], I'm sorry for what I did. [Go into it in whatever detail feels good to you.] I was doing my best at the time. I love you. Can we move on together?"

Listen.

Take five to ten deep breaths.

If you wish to ask for forgiveness, do it now.

Say, "I love you. Thank you. I've got you."

I challenge you, the next time you want to put yourself down, to whip out the picture of little you and tell him or her the words you're telling yourself in your own mind. Is it fair to him or her? If it's not, stop.

Repeat, "I love you. Thank you. I've got you." Say it as many times as necessary to soothe the both of you.

Open your eyes. Kiss or hug the photo. Keep it somewhere close so you can do this again.

Now write down some of the thoughts you have when you see this photo and respond to it this way.

And don't let your sweet younger self down, okay? She or he deserves your love and forgiveness. *No matter what. Read that again.*

> **DIRECT MESSAGE**
>
> You can create a Childhood Picture Posse with a couple of friends who'd benefit from regular reminders to love themselves. I created this idea after a friend left an emotionally abusive relationship. I asked her to text a picture of herself as a kid to me (in the photo she's holding a bird on her arm, and it's adorable). And every now and then, at random times, I'll text her that picture with a simple message: a reminder to love that girl today. Now a few of us girls do it because there's nothing like the powerful reminder that *you* deserve your love. Try it!

Loving Yourself Today

At the age of four, living in poverty-stricken postwar Poland in the 1940s, my mom was in a house fire. It left her with a permanent burn mark on her face and her left arm. The Danish Red Cross, who were posted nearby, saved her life. They gave her a white plastic face mask to keep her little face together. She was spoon-fed. Her brother was scared of her, as were all the children in the neighborhood.

The permanent scarring on her face made her feel ugly, especially as she grew into her teenage years and became interested in boys. I have every sympathy. It was a big burn scar on her *face*! When she spoke to a boy, the burn mark on her left cheek would blush bright red and feel hot — so she avoided speaking to boys altogether. My mom concentrated on being the best at school, thinking, *If I can't be pretty, I'll be smart.*

Later, she moved to England to learn English, and then spent her life as a teacher and volunteer in places like Ghana and Zimbabwe. Today, now in her seventies, she's content with her life. After a lifetime of challenges as a single mother and having done lots of inner work, she feels good about herself (and still volunteers at a local school, where they call her "Granny").

But she tells her five daughters, "I wish someone had told me I was special, that I was pretty, that I could love myself." It took her many years to know she could give *herself* this gift. And she often repeats, *If I could live my life over again, knowing what I know now, things would be so different…* Most important, she'd start approving of herself, scars included, far sooner.

I asked my mother what enabled her to take this turn in her life, from feeling very unloved as a child to being full of self-love today. She didn't ascribe this perspective shift to any one moment, but she did choose to share some thoughts about how she came to love herself so well, and I want to share them here with you, too, because I think they're really valuable:

- She reads all the time. Her heroes are Lincoln, Franklin, Einstein, Washington, Churchill, and many others, and she's always learning about them and trying to apply their lessons to her own life.
- She's come to believe that it's wisdom, not wealth or looks, that gets you through life successfully.
- No one can make you happy, she says. You are happy because you are a loving person.

Borrowing from Shakespeare, my mother talks about her "crown of contentment" that she's hammered and polished over the years. She says she doesn't wear it on her head but keeps it in her heart. It's a plain crown, without precious stones, crowns that plenty of kings can't have. She says that while she is not wealthy, she has made her own crown, which means that one day, she will die *rich*.

Her ability to find true self-love began with her acknowledging what she's been through. And what a strong, competent, and kind woman she is. But how great would it have been for her to have gotten there a little sooner?

Consider this for a second: anyone who lives to eighty-five gets one thousand months of life on earth.

I'm thirty-five right now. If I'm mega lucky and live till age eighty-five, I've already lived well over one-third of my years. That's fifty summers left, fifty more Christmases with my husband (if we're both lucky), and fifty more springs blossoming to life in Central Park. Not so many when you pause and calculate, right?

Self-approval is nothing to wait for. Do it now.

Check this:

❏ Stop complaining about yourself, immediately. No exceptions allowed.
❏ Practice affirmative mirror talk at every opportunity.
❏ Write down your Twelve Magic Moments, and review them often.
❏ Practice Loving Little Me whenever you need to.
❏ Create a Childhood Picture Posse if it feels good!

CHAPTER SIX

It's Okay If
People Don't Like You

Haters are confused admirers.

PAULO COELHO

When I was a teenager, I was a counselor for my younger peers every Friday at lunchtime. One late-summer day a petite girl came to me in tears, rubbing her red nose and looking at the floor.

"What's up, Tina?" I asked, touching her shoulder as she sat down.

"Jenna said I'm a copycat," she blurted. "That I try to just look and sound like her. *I don't!*"

I understood well the stab of pain you feel when someone criticizes or betrays you. "Oh," I said. "Did she just say this to you?" I was willing to bring Jenna in and mediate a little.

"No! She didn't tell me. Claire did. She told everyone last Friday at a sleepover."

It was Thursday. Nearly week-old news. But teary Tina had just found out.

I listened for a little while and tried to make light of it. "It's okay, Tina. It's normal to feel this way — it hurts! Let me ask you something. What if Jenna said you were a bird. Would she be right?"

Tina remained straight-faced.

"What about a car, a tree, a pair of scissors?"

Tina brightened up a little. She understood what I was getting at. She was attaching so much meaning to an opinion — and an absolute falsehood! — someone else had voiced about her.

An opinion coming out of someone else's mouth can't hurt you. And it doesn't even have to mean anything. This was Jenna's problem, not Tina's. And what the Jennas of the world say and do is not our business, right? And it's certainly nothing the Tinas can control.

I also pointed out that Jenna had said this more than a week ago. "That's ages!" I told her. "It's old news. You didn't hear about it then, and you were fine. What's changed?"

I saw a little *aha!* moment happen within her as her shoulders straightened and her eyes opened. Could something Claire blurted out on the playground *make* her cry? No!

Tina was making herself cry by:

- paying attention to criticism/hearsay (best avoided in the first place when possible)
- thinking another person's opinions mean something (unless they're coming from a loving place, they don't)
- continuing to think about that opinion (which is 100 percent optional)

How often do we take critical statements to heart? Multiple times a day, in some cases. I learned something interesting on Joel Osteen's podcast recently, something that can boost anyone's immunity to haters. It's what the term *offense* means, originally in Greek. It means "bait." Yep — bait! And you're taking it over and over again, every time someone offends you. They dangle, you bite. And you let it happen whenever your fishy friends (or strangers on the internet, even) feel like trawling.

Does this simple exchange among children highlight how powerful we are to reject (and simply remain neutral to) criticism? Criticism *can't hurt you*. It's an illusion! The thing that hurts is the bad feeling you allow to remain in your body when you pay attention to that feeling. And the good news is that it's up to you. Are you going to choose to punish yourself?

Consider this. A snakebite can kill you, right? Wrong! The venom left over in your body does. And that's on you to release, metaphorically speaking.

What venom are you carrying around? An unkind comment on your boss outfit from an acquaintance five months ago? A snub on what should have been a well-earned promotion from a jealous manager? A bitchy comment or secret revealed behind your back that sparked a texting frenzy?

If there's one thing you take away from this book, I hope it's this. What someone says about you is 100 percent — with no exceptions — about them. Let me illustrate this in two ways.

When I turned thirty, I wrote a column on thirty life lessons I'd learned. As I was putting the lessons together, I asked my friends about the biggest lesson they'd learned by the age of thirty. Here's a mishmash of what I heard:

- No carbs after 2:00 PM.
- Get life insurance when you're young.

- Don't put up with a boss you hate for long.
- Use a body brush to exfoliate, and always swipe up toward the heart.
- You don't have to have kids.

Now let me give you a small insight into each person who gave these statements:

- No carbs after 2:00 PM. — From a former fitness model.
- Get life insurance when you're young. — From a wealth-building, financially savvy investor.
- Don't put up with a boss you hate for long. — From my rebel entrepreneur friend.
- Use a body brush to exfoliate, and always swipe up toward the heart. — From a beauty blogger.
- You don't have to have kids. — From an awesome non-mom friend who lives life her way.

What do all these pieces of advice have in common? They are all about the people giving them! We see the world as *we* are. It's madly subjective. It's like the Marcus Aurelius quote: "Everything we hear is an opinion, not a fact. Everything we see is a perspective, not the truth." (My thirty-lessons-learned piece resonated, too. Paulo Coelho, author of *The Alchemist*, shared it with his millions of social media followers and even published it on his blog — I freaked out when that happened.)

Here is another good example of this dynamic. My sister was planning to move to Dubai for two years for her husband's job and was a bit nervous about moving to a new place. This is what her friends had to say:

- That's very brave — isn't it dangerous in the Middle East?
- That's so cool. Wow! Imagine all the different foods and flavors there.
- Get X and Y vaccinations before you go.

Let's take a look at who her pals are:

- That's very brave — isn't it dangerous in the Middle East? — From her friend who'd never left England.
- That's so cool. Wow! Imagine all the different foods and flavors there. — From her passionate foodie friend.
- Get X and Y vaccinations before you go. — From her nurse friend.

So what does this tell you about *anyone* who tells you anything, let alone who criticizes you? It's got nothing to do with *you*. People are constantly confirming their own biases.

And consider this. The worst thing that criticism can do to you is make you feel bad for a period of time (how long is up to you). Guess who can reverse that? Yep, you. Your ensuing negative thoughts were created in your mind, and they can be destroyed the same way.

Let It Pass

A large part of self-approval is just being *willing* to experience negative emotions. That's what all self-approving, self-confident people do differently. They're not as put off or scared by temporary, unhappy emotions, like being embarrassed or uncomfortable, or even being disliked or ridiculed by someone. They're willing to let it happen. The most confident among us are even willing to look stupid or be wrong. Because the worst that can happen is a bad feeling within for a while. So what? It'll pass. Unless someone is holding a gun to your head, you're fine. You're safe. Breathe. Feelings are temporary.

Can you imagine what your life would be like if you were more willing to go there with uncomfortable feelings? If someone not liking or approving of you didn't faze you all that much? You'd be unstoppable. As a columnist, I've received a lot of hate online. Here are some of the ugliest things that have been said about me:

"What a gold-digging whore!"

"She has to be sleeping with someone to be earning so much money!"

"I can't believe this random girl gets paid to write this crap."

"Your husband's a pussy."

"Your training is taking way too long. I wanted to kill myself watching it."

(This last one was a live comment I got when I was giving a free online workshop. I sure hope she wasn't harmed!)

Is something becoming clear here?

The internet (and the world) is a weird place! Other people's opinions of you and their words *don't* have to touch you. And you do *not* have to set anyone straight. I took a line from the Bible on this one: Jesus responded to his critics "not even a word." He understood that what other people say about you doesn't matter. It's like he was the original #zerofucks guy! High five, Jesus.

Let this give you a lot of peace. You never have to defend yourself. That's not your job. Your worthiness as a human is not deletable, ever. No matter who says what about you. So if you wish, write an email to a person who hurt you, but don't press Send. Shout, "You mean-ass troll!" in your living room to that person, who won't hear it. Or scream into a pillow to let your anger and frustration pass. Breathe. Let some time pass. Remember that your feelings are hurt now, yes. But just like the clouds passing in the sky, they are temporary.

> **DIRECT MESSAGE**
>
> If you can help it, never, ever defend yourself. Ever. Someone once said in an online comment to me, when I was speaking of the okay-ness of divorce, "You seem like a real bitch!" I responded (couldn't help it this time), "Yeah, you're probably right about that. Call my ex-husband, he'd agree!" Nothing takes the wind outta someone's sails like being defenseless. It's disarming to them. Even annoying. Try it! You might get addicted.

When You're Left Out

Even being left out doesn't have to hurt you. I remember a time a text from my friend Kat popped up on my screen: "Are you going to Andrew's party?"

I thought, *Yes! Probably*. Then I returned to my conversation with my dinner date, Ava. As Ava and I were wrapping up, she said, "You're coming to Andrew's party, right?" and I answered confidently again, "Probably!" But as we parted ways, I checked my in-box for the Paperless Post invite. Nothing. A Facebook invite, then? I scrolled through my notifications — nope. Hmmm. Could I have been...left out? It sunk in. Yep, that was it.

Ouch.

I thought about it for the rest of the evening and the following day. I considered texting Andrew to ask what was up, but my pride wouldn't let me. It stung, but this happens to all of us at one time or another: we get left out of a party, project, heck — even a group text chain.

It never feels good, but does it really have to bother us so much? Nope. Look — you can accept that it doesn't feel great. Because denying that something bothers us only makes it linger longer. I had a mini vent to Heath, who's levelheaded, and he said, "Who cares? I wouldn't go all the way to Connecticut for a party anyway!"

His response landed with me because it was actually true. While I wanted to be included — who doesn't! — I probably *wouldn't* have wanted to make the trek, or I might have made up an excuse as to why I couldn't go when it came down to it. Yes, I was miffed, and in truth, my feelings were hurt. But the sting diminished when I actually thought about it: I probably wouldn't have wanted to go anyway. In the end, Andrew did me a favor.

Does being left out of something make you (irrationally) think you want it more than you actually do? Be honest, now. We usually want what we don't have a little more, right?

Consider: *Am I Being Left Out on Purpose?*

One year I had an intimate birthday dinner at Soho House in NYC. They can seat only eight people at their biggest table. So I chose seven people who all knew one another pretty well. I thought, *I can see and celebrate with other people separately!* A couple of Insta snaps I was tagged in later, and I had a couple of snarky texts from friends who weren't there. In cases like these, I find an honest explanation usually helps. Assumptions are dangerous. Clarity is good!

Being the perceived "rejector" in this instance, I felt bad that other people felt left out, but it helped me see that "rejection" for what it is: nothing! It's almost always not intentional or malicious. Life just has a lotta moving parts, and we make many on-the-spot, not-at-all-deep decisions. It's not always a big deal. Chill.

Think: *Am I Overreacting?*

In many cases, our emotions *aren't rational*. I once had a coworker, Daniel, who was obsessing over the thought of getting fired when he was left out of a particular project at work. He kept asking me, "Do they have it in for me, or what? My clients are involved in this. Why aren't I in the meetings?"

I didn't have the answer, but my gut told me that Daniel was being over-the-top with his response, and I told him that. Soon after, his boss invited him to step in and help manage the project. He explained that he was concerned that Daniel had too much on his plate so he'd been trying to shield him from the new endeavor for as long as he could.

Daniel's boss was actually protecting him because he cared for him as an important team member who was stretched too thin already.

What a sigh of relief — and a mini eye roll at the old panic brain, right?

DIRECT MESSAGE

It's much easier to see things objectively when they happen to someone else. If I were Daniel, I probably would have been freaking out, too! In fact, when anything bad happens to someone else, we can see it more clearly, like, "Oh, that celebrity didn't have her talk show renewed, but she'll find a more suitable home. She rocks!" versus when we ourselves are let go from a job or project: "I'm such a loser, my life and career are over. I might as well die."

The next time something unwanted happens, picture it happening to someone else for a second. How serious is it then? You almost never worry about their life being over, right? You know they'll be okay. The same goes for you.

Once you feel left out, it's easy to stay mad at the person who hurt you. But after you acknowledge that being left out doesn't feel good and assess your reaction, think:

- Does this experience teach me anything?
- Do I need to speak up more?
- Do I need to question my assumptions?
- Do I need to ask for what I want more often?
- Do I need to find some new friends if the same people keep hurting my feelings?

If we let them, painful parts of our lives can become gorgeous shifts in a new direction — the old blessing in disguise in action. That's what I think about when I think about Andrew, who I haven't seen for a while. There's no harm or hate here. It's all good! And we live in a busy world, so that just means more time for the people who matter most to me, even if we're not all at every party, every time.

Outclassing the Haters

Think about it. The feeling of being hated by someone or of being left out doesn't have to stay with you. Even physical pain is temporary, and when you can breathe and relax a little, it passes sooner. Dale Carnegie said, "No one kicks a dead dog," and he was right. People attack and hate the movers and shakers. They criticize the people who are brave enough to stand out in this judgmental world.

Hate is not the opposite of love; the opposite of love is pure indifference. If no one cared about you, they'd say nothing about you. If they're talking 'bout you — they care. Damn — you're popular! And this kind of sentiment doesn't apply just to our social lives, either: I learned this cool business lesson while working in tech sales. Often a potential client will ask, "Who are your main competitors?" This is a way for them to understand where you fit into your industry's ecosystem.

But it's also a way to place you in a bucket — fast.

Many sellers are quick to mention bigwig competitors, like Google and Facebook, to make themselves look good and then throw in a couple of smaller players that probably more closely resemble their true status. They then proceed to highlight each of their competitor's flaws and dissect their offerings. It can get very detailed. It becomes a weird ode to the people you do *not* want your client thinking about! *And it doesn't make you look any better*. Same as if you spilled coffee on a rival's T-shirt. That doesn't make your T-shirt look any cuter!

I learned to *never* mention a competitor's name. Like... ever. Not once! I'd say something like, "Well, that's a great question, but tricky to answer because we're the only platform who [*list impressive stuff here and go into an ode about your damn self*]." I learned from a great, seasoned salesperson that you don't want to give even one second of airtime to your competition. Why speak their name at all?

The same applies in life, right?

If your name is coming out of someone else's mouth at a lunch you don't even know about, well. Who needs a teleporting machine? You're the girl of the hour without even being there! Lucky you! You should start worrying about the day people *stop* hating you, in fact. You will have lost your edge. Zero bitchy comments? *This cannot be happening!*

DIRECT MESSAGE

Have you ever watched *The Bachelor* or *The Bachelor-ette*? Any contender who spends their precious limited time with the coveted bachelor or bachelorette talking about the other guys or girls in the competition (and how obnoxious/self-centered/aggressive/fill-in-the-blank they are) rarely makes it to the end.

In their complaining/hatred/gossiping about other people, they themselves become more suspicious and un-likable. Focus on yo' self, singletons!

I became painfully aware of the force of hatred early on in my side gig; I believe the universe gave this awareness to me as a gift. I was interviewing Kris Jenner (matriarch of the Kardashian/Jenner family) for *Marie Claire*. We had a fun-filled, hour-long conversation. She was delightful, funny, and full of advice, including this nugget about overcoming criticism: "It's sad that there are people somewhere hiding behind their computers and writing cruel things about others on social networks."

Given her fame, the piece was crazy popular, and she tweeted it from her account. When she tweeted, she tagged @marieclaire and @susiemoore. Because I was tagged, I was notified of all the comments. Every. Single. One. Ninety percent of them were mean. And by mean, I'm telling you…*yikes*. I've never seen such bitter words in my life. Remember that guy who said I looked like a man in my YouTube video? He has *nothing* on the people who were throwing vitriol at Kris. People wanted her kids dead. Someone said all her daughters were pigs (or did lewd things with pigs). The world can be mean.

What you don't read or hear can't bother you, though. (Hey — did someone say *Stop Checking Your Likes*?) Unless it's from your boss, a loving parent, or someone else you look up to and accept input from, avoid hearing feedback at all if you can. I remember one crisp autumn evening when I was at a fancy art gallery opening for the free wine (we were in our budget-strapped-new-to-NYC stage, and we took in as much free stuff as we could). As I tucked into a shrimp satay stick I heard a woman in a bright-pink dress whisper to her friend in a polka-dot dress, "Hey, I wasn't gonna say anything, but one of the other moms told me about Jake's —"

But she was cut off before she could finish.

Jake's what? Jake must be her son, right? Even I wanted to know. *Who is Jake, and what is he doing?!* See? Gossip is seductive!

"I don't really want to talk about Jake's issue tonight. Thanks, though, Becca," she replied, touching her arm warmly.

Polka-dot woman then excused herself. As she walked toward the bathroom I could almost see her flicking imaginary dust off her shoulder. Great job, polka dots! You kept it classy.

No matter how hard you try, though, there'll be times when you do hear stuff, and it will upset you — at least for a short time. Like the time a friend of mine had some bad publicity around his business. He was upset, got his lawyer involved, and got so worked up that it was causing stress for his entire team. He called me a couple of days after it happened. I told him that if I were him, I would leave it alone altogether. Drop it. Delete it from memory. Bury it! "This will naturally get buried with other press over time...*so what?*"

"And don't hit back!" I affirmed. I reminded him what Jesus said. (Hard to argue with Jesus, eh?)

"People only throw stones at trees that have fruit," I told him, quoting the old saying. "So, congrats, ya juicy apple tree. You're worth a rock attack."

Here are some hateful comments, the likes of which we've all heard before (sometimes shared as "opinions"). Let's interpret them in a new way:

Sara is so full of herself = I envy Sara's easy confidence.

Todd snaked his way up the corporate ladder = Todd has something going for him that I don't have (and I want it), and it triggers me. I'm fascinated by Todd.

That girl had all the lucky breaks = I'm not satisfied with my station, and I don't feel like I'm enough. Deep down I know she's just braver than me. And pretty brilliant.

Lisa is fake = How is it possible for someone to have it all, and also be so nice?

Zach is so overhyped = I wish I were not so lazy and could get off my ass and do half as much stuff as Zach does.

She's too thin/Botoxed/made-up/tarty/tattooed = I am not happy with how I look, and I think about looks a whole lot.

Sam is so arrogant = How does Sam believe in himself so much? Can I buy a jar of that somewhere?

My boss is stupid = I'm frustrated at myself for being in this position in my career. I know I'm better than this.

How is this person famous for doing nothing? = I should be getting more credit for my life and my contribution.

She comes from money = I'm not sure I can achieve the same level of success without family connections or money.

Can you see that some of these comments are a form of caring — admiration, even? And it's a pure, direct reflection of the person offering the judgment.

And any judgment itself is arrogant. Who is to judge how to live your life but you? Your life belongs to you. You came into this world alone, and you'll exit it alone. Everything in between is also up to you...alone. So you can leave people who don't like you alone, too.

Check this:

- [ ] The next time you feel hurt by someone, don't think, *What's wrong with me?* Think instead, *What's happened to this person? Maybe this isn't even about me at all? Am I making up a story about this in my head?*
- [ ] The next time you feel left out, think, *Am I overreacting? Is this really a big deal?*
- [ ] Stop gossiping. It never feels good for long. And the people you gossip with are likely to be gossiping about you, too.
- [ ] If some people in your life keep hurting your feelings, commit to forming new friendships.

CHAPTER SEVEN

See the World through Comedy-Colored Glasses

*Heraclitus would shed tears whenever he went out
in public — Democritus laughed. One saw the whole as a
parade of miseries, the other of follies. And so, we should
take a lighter view of things and bear them with an easy spirit,
for it is more human to laugh at life than to lament it.*

SENECA, *On Tranquility of Mind*

One day after school when I was fifteen or sixteen, my dad wouldn't let me into his house. *That's strange*, I thought. His car was there. And when I leaned into the glass pane of the door closely, I heard hushed voices inside. I was confused. He knew I always came over after school. I remember the weight of my Caterpillar backpack, which I was desperate to throw on the sofa. It was drizzling outside (hey, it was England) and my clothes were starting to get damp. All day long, I'd been looking forward to digging into the caramel ice cream I'd hidden at the back of the freezer. And maybe even smoking a little pot. It was a tradition in my teenage life. Often my friends and I would go to my dad's house after school. Eat, chill, sometimes smoke. My dad would give us all a copy of a Shakespeare play and make us read parts as characters he'd assigned us. He'd chastise us for emphasizing the wrong words. One time my friend Kate was Desdemona in *Othello* and said after an entire act, "I didn't even get to say anything that time!" "Ah, good, onto the next scene!" my dad boomed. (I wanted to punch her for prolonging the acting.)

In hindsight, it was a good thing that I had walked home alone. I knocked at the door with my fist again and then graduated my assault to the more fragile window (it had been broken and replaced a few times already — whenever we locked ourselves out). I peered in the precarious glass square. And behind another door with stained glass, I saw a figure moving. It didn't look like my dad. It looked...like a tall woman.

Was someone, was she...naked in there?

Yuck.

I felt gross all of a sudden and in an instant stepped back. I thought that maybe I could just get some chocolate and ciggies from the corner store as a consolation (and to escape this weird situation). In that instant, my sheepish dad arrived at the door, in an off-white waffle bathrobe. I'd never seen the robe before. The whole scenario was out of place in the bright daylight (behind him was darkness, with all the curtains drawn).

"What do you want?" he asked, as if I were a door-to-door seller, not his daughter.

"What do I *want*? Let me in!" I demanded.

I couldn't connect the dots. My dad loved female attention, but as far as I knew he had no girlfriend at the moment. Who was inside with him? At that moment, a blond woman wearing a long T-shirt came up behind him and said, "Hi, I'm Tracy!"

I smiled weakly back. I couldn't stop staring at the frosted blue shadow on her eyelids. (Blue? Is this the eighties, woman?!) Her smile didn't reach her eyes.

Then I heard a husky voice whisper, "And I'm Karen," and my attention moved behind them to the brunette standing at the bottom of the stairs. There were two women with him. I sidestepped my dad and Tracy and went into the house.

There was silence. But oddly, I don't remember it being especially awkward. It was my house, and I wanted them gone. My dad (who could never handle confrontation) climbed upstairs and slammed the bedroom door, upset with me.

Oh. *Aha!*

It hit me like a wave — the way that only truth can. *These women were prostitutes.* My mom always told me he had a penchant for them. One had stolen his watch when they were living and teaching in Africa, and another gave him a sexually transmitted disease scare. I had heard the stories. But it was still a surprise to see them in living color myself.

"We're friends of your dad," Karen offered. "We're about to leave anyway." Then they both scurried upstairs, no doubt where they had been quite busy before my arrival.

"Okay." I shrugged.

I busied myself in the kitchen, scoping out the ice cream situation and looking for the pot that we kept hidden in a Fisherman's Friend tin.

They took a few minutes up there. I heard footsteps back and forth, and some incomprehensible mumblings. I made out the words *cash* and *camera*, and that was it. I grimaced (I was young but not naive) but otherwise felt oddly neutral about the weird situation.

Minutes later, Tracy and Karen walked out the front door — the barrier between us just moments before — with weak smiles and even weaker waves. Was I feeling a bit sorry for them? It was hard to attach a precise word to my feelings. They seemed old to me back then (they were perhaps in their thirties or forties).

It was the last I'd ever see of my dad's "friends." Thirty minutes or so later, probably compelled by the smell of weed and the sound of the whistling kettle, my dad came downstairs (minus one skanky robe and plus one polo shirt and ironed trousers).

In silence, I handed him the joint I was smoking and pulled out an extra mug from the kitchen cupboard. "The ice cream's finished," I said. My punishment to him for the inconvenience of the afternoon. He raised his eyebrows in indifference. We sat down, him on his leather La-Z-Boy, me cross-legged on the sofa. As usual, all was forgotten fast with my sometimes smug, completely unpredictable, eccentric father.

"So, *Susan*. What did the teachers *think* they taught you at school today?" he asked. And in a second, it became like every other day.

At school the next day, I told a couple of my friends who knew my dad, and they thought it was *shocking*. I thought it was weird (and kinda gross), for sure. But also, pretty funny. It was just my crazy-ass dad. In fact, everyone loved him and loved coming over to his place, where traditional parenting rules never seemed to apply.

My pal Chris said, "I love that there were not one, but *two* hookers in there!" We had a good laugh about it. The laughter lasted for months. It's amazing how nonjudgmental young people can be.

Lighten Up

Can we throw on some comedy-colored shades and lighten up a little? And just not take everything so seriously? Life isn't meant to be one great big white-knuckle ride. It can be a hilarious adventure. It's not something to be endured until you make it to the bitter end, hopefully as unscathed as possible. I love what Joan Rivers said: "Life goes by fast. Enjoy it. Calm down. It's all funny. Next. Everyone gets so upset about the wrong things."

Guess what? Death has a 100 percent success rate. It's coming for all of us. The next time you need a reality check, go to the graveyard. I'm being serious. I love cemeteries. They remind me that everything is temporary. Right now, a picture of a beautiful church cemetery in England is the screensaver on my phone, so that the next time I want to freak out because I have to wait *a full seven minutes* for a subway train, those weather-beaten, eighteenth-century headstones can bring me back to earth.

Side bonus: you can always get a parking space in a cemetery.

Alain de Botton, founder of the School of Life in London, says, "One of the things that I think we should all do a lot more is put skulls on our desks. In the Middle Ages and the early Modern period, a vital piece of interior design was a skull.... A skull was something you'd always put on your desk. And the reason for that is that as you were doing your work, you'd always look at the skull and think, 'I'm gonna be like him in a little while.'"

Why do I agree with this so strongly?

1. On a very literal level, it's the truth. We *will* look like him in a little while, and that fact can be sobering
2. It's perspective, in an instant. There's nothing like a skull to remind you of your own temporary existence and to light a fire under your ass.

In fact, death and regret are two of my favorite things to think and talk about. They are life affirming. Death is on its way for us all, and it comes without an appointment. But regrets don't have to.

Remember: anyone who lives to eighty-five gets one thousand months of life.

That time my bestie, Alexis, and I were looking at decades-old photos of ourselves, ruing our self-criticism? Well, the sooner we learn to appreciate what we're rockin' in the moment, the better. My mother-in-law recently told me she was looking at photos of herself with her three kids from thirty years ago. At the time the photos were taken, she told me that she remembers feeling, *I'm so overwhelmed! I'm not doing a good job!* But now she wishes she had thought, *Look at my figure! I was a fun mom! I was in my prime*! Will you be thinking something like this in your later years?

If so, what the heck are you worrying about and taking so seriously today? My mom always says, "I'm over seventy, darling; nothing bothers me." I love this about her. Because it reminds me that age can naturally deliver this kind of attitude. But do we have to wait until we're over seventy? I don't think so. But we do unconsciously, a lot of the time.

Observe 90 percent of people out there for a second. The morning commuters frowning into their phones. The sharp, stern faces of women in any workout class ("Crack a smile guys, it's only barre!" a teacher I dig once said). The solemn-looking conversations in any boardroom or coffee shop you walk by.

There's an old statistic that circulates saying something along the lines of *the average four-year-old laughs three hundred times a day. The average forty-year-old? Only four.* It might be inaccurate, but the gist of the message *is* accurate. We've all become a bit uptight, anxious, afraid, and tense, haven't we? And it's ruining us. It's sapping not only our day-to-day energy but our creativity and imagination, too. And stress is killing our health.

When I was a teenage waitress, the café owner I worked for had a rule that whenever we accidentally smashed a plate or glass, we'd laugh! It was an excellent policy. And he ran a very successful small business. No surprise there! We could relax and be ourselves at work — and not fret over making mistakes (which happen everywhere, in every business, every day). We all wanted to be there, and that energy attracted customers.

I was reminded of this when Heath and I were in Paris on a summer vacation several years ago. We were eating dinner at our favorite steak frites restaurant, Le Relais de l'Entrecôte, just off the Champs-Élysées. As we were finishing our steak frites (which is world famous...and pretty much the only thing on the menu) and a bottle of Bordeaux, I was recounting a funny story to Heath. I can't recall exactly what it was about, but it evidently required excessive gesticulation, which resulted in me spilling my red wine all over the guy sitting next to me who, *to my horror*, was wearing all white! Aaaall. White.

Then there was an impossibly long and incredibly awkward moment of silence. The kind where you wish there was a window you could jump out of.

Then all of a sudden the man...burst into *laughter*! Thank God! We apologized profusely and offered to pay for his dinner and give him some money for dry cleaning (or a new shirt!). *"Ne vous inquiétez pas à ce sujet! Ne vous inquiétez pas à ce sujet!* (Don't worry about it, don't worry about it!)," he said.

Overcome with embarrassment, we quickly paid for our

meal and ran out the door. Then, as we were walking briskly as far away from the restaurant as we could get, we heard someone shout out, "*Mademoiselle! Attendre!* (Miss! Wait!)" I turned around and saw it was the guy from the restaurant, running down the street after us. I could see him more clearly under the streetlamps now. People in the street were staring at him, since it looked as though he'd been stabbed with a knife in the stomach.

"*Tu as oublié quelque chose!* (You forgot something!)" He handed me the denim jacket I had left behind in my scurry, then ran back up the street. A good sense of humor and kindness. What a cool man.

Happiness and Humor

In his bestselling book *The Happiness Advantage*, happiness researcher Shawn Achor explains it best: "Success orbits around happiness, not the other way around." His research shows that a happy disposition and a happy work environment are the foundations of a successful career and life. We tend to believe that success leads to happiness, when in fact, it's the other way around. It's like we're all walking around just waiting for something to happen. Or for something to become clear so our life can properly begin. But when we live like this, we're missing the point.

In this precise moment, your life is in process, and it's rushing by you. In this precise moment. This clarity is available to you every single second that you're breathing. *This very moment is your life!*

Not long ago, I was pacing my apartment cursing the ceiling (loudly) because I accidentally had sent a newsletter out with an incorrect link and then had to issue an apology — and a correction — to the more than 130,000 people on my email list. If you were a fly on the wall, you would have thought I was having a heart attack. But what happened?

Nothing. Someone even emailed me saying, "Good to know you're human and not a robot, dude!"

When you see the world through comedy-colored glasses, nothing can hold you down for long. Even death. My dad would refuse hospitalization in his darkest, most addicted spirals almost any time he could. He'd say, "I am going to die with a beautiful woman on top of me — not in a bloody hospital bed!" It still makes me laugh to think of it (nearly two decades years later).

My mom also has a great sense of humor, despite her difficult past. She laughs (and sings!) more than anyone I know, in her native Polish. My sisters and I break out Polish tunes once in a while to make each other laugh. I also like to throw around the Polish swear words to shock my mom (she says she "feels the words" in Polish but I can say whatever words I like all day long in English and she doesn't mind).

What are you taking too seriously? Almost everything bad that happens is 99 percent less serious than you think. Next time a plan goes awry, can you try to find the comedy in the tragedy? This is easier in theory and harder in practice, I know. But it's possible and gets easier the more we do it. In every moment we can look for a reason to laugh instead of a reason to be offended.

Humor is the key to improving a lot of perceived concerns in our lives. It's the remedy to many tough situations. And in a lot of cases, it accelerates healing and results. Seeing the humor in things is not to be confused with having an unhealthy denial of real pain. When we need help, we need help. But an ability to be lighter about our worries puts people, events, and the future into perspective. And what is our "stuff," exactly? It's the thoughts we think, which over time become our beliefs. And our beliefs typically define the way we live.

The good news is, a thought can be changed; it loses its power when it's questioned. For example, a friend of mine grew up with a dad who told her, "Rich people are greedy — they're all crooks" and "Money is the root of all evil." Okay. That's a dominant thought in some homes. Is it a fact? Let's see. Sure, you can find plenty of evidence to support it if you want to. But aren't some poor people crooks, too? Do money and morality *have* to have a direct correlation? Perhaps not. Isn't money also the root of all philanthropy? Of much generosity? Of cool vacations?

You don't have to be rich to be greedy or commit a crime or be cruel to someone.

Some of my dad's drug-dealing friends (some of whom were addicts themselves) had no money whatsoever. They lived day-to-day, and some days they didn't even eat. And they stole from people sometimes. They got into blowout brawls in the local pubs (one stabbed a rival drug dealer, who fell into a coma, and ended up in jail for attempted murder).

So maybe we can invite this questioning into all our thoughts. Eckhart Tolle said something that bowled me over once: "Here's a great spiritual practice for you — don't take your thoughts too seriously." Just because we think something negative doesn't mean that it's true. It's hard to do this, though, when we have thought loops on repeat for, in some cases, *years.*

"Is That a Fact?"

I've been wildly inspired by Byron Katie's teachings called The Work, which helps us pretty much dissolve almost every perceived tragedy (including death) by using simple questioning into our truth. Just as Eckhart says, we don't have to buy into every thought we have *just because it's there.*

I've worked with clients who have even burst into laughter — yep, *the magic stuff*! — when questioning what they believe to be true. Together we question their feelings and thoughts about their issues and explore whether they are facts or theory. The differentiation matters more than you might believe. Even if it's something that's been making them miserable as a "fact" for years. We play around with it. See if it's actually real.

A friend of mine, Andi, has compared herself (harshly) to her sister for years. It doesn't seem to matter what she's comparing: dress size, amount of money in the bank, amount of attention received from their mother, number of Facebook friends…the list is exhaustive. She always evaluates her life based on her sister's progress. One Sunday morning, we were sharing a beautiful brunch outside at Tavern on the Green in Central Park. It was a perfect spring day, the mimosas were flowing, and I'd just taken a bite from my big, gorgeous plate of eggs Benedict, when she put her fork down and blurted out, "I'm getting frustrated in my small apartment. My sister has a bigger home — I need something more like that."

Andi *doesn't* have a small place by most New York standards — she has a two-bedroom apartment in a swanky Manhattan neighborhood. But it's seldom about the actual circumstances when it comes to comparison craziness. In fact, I remember reading not long ago about how (and I'm paraphrasing) we'd rather earn $80,000 if our college peers earned $50,000 versus making $100,000 if all our peers were making $150,000. Because it's not the number, it's the rank on the metaphorical ladder. We'd rather make *less money* as long as it's *more than* our pals. Nuts, right?

Anyway, I took this opportunity to see if it was a fact that Andi needed a bigger home. I took a sip of my mimosa and said, "Andi, your place is too small for you? I mean, is that a fact?"

"Yep!" she answered without a second thought, testing a shishito pepper to determine its spiciness level (they're made to trick you!).

"Okay," I responded. "Your two-bedder that you live in solo in this pretty pricey neighborhood. It's a fact that it's too small for you?"

She looked up and thought for a moment. Silence ensued.

"Well, hmmm. Most people live in a lot smaller spaces around here, I guess. It's pretty nice to have an office at home. Oh, man, I sound ungrateful, don't I?" she asked, putting down her fork.

"Not at all — this is just thinking about it a little more!" I said soothingly. "Hey, can I ask what else is going through your head when you believe the 'fact' that your apartment's too small?"

"That I'm a failure. My sister went into law *and* married a lawyer. No wonder she has a huge-ass townhouse!"

Ah. Now we were getting somewhere. This wasn't about *her* apartment's square footage at all.

I then threw in my other favorite questions. I just couldn't resist — it almost always cracks the case wide open! *"What else?"*

"I feel behind at life. I want a husband. I feel like life isn't fair to me. And...I don't even want freakin' stairs in my house. I hate stairs!"

We both laughed. Oh, the sweet relief of laughter when thoughts that once drove us crazy start to seem ludicrous. *Andi didn't even want a townhouse.* Her initial statement was already starting to feel, frankly, a little bloody silly, really.

"What if this faulty fact you've had on repeat in your mind — that you need a bigger place — was no longer active?" I asked.

"Oh, man." She shook her head, a million new thoughts hitting her at once. "Happy! Free! I'd buy some new plants, probably! I'd make my bed. I'd enjoy my cute bar area and even cook for a guy there, maybe. I haven't done that in a while. I'd probably even go visit my sister more often and bring her kid a toy or something."

Do you see how questioning our thoughts can reveal some real stuff? And even make us more loving? Thoughts and feeling are *not* facts!

DIRECT MESSAGE

The next time a troubling thought crops up or plays on loop, ask yourself:

Is this a fact or a theory? What if it were no longer active?

The best part here is that what stays active is 100 percent yours to control. In a world where many things cannot be controlled — the weather, the traffic, who your parents are, and so on — you get to love or lose the "facts" you find!

The Fact-Finding Method

Here's an example of how we can do some useful fact-finding in everyday life: We start by questioning *the factual nature* of any statement in order to gain immediate perspective.

"I don't have enough money."

Is that a fact?

Have you not eaten in days? Are you genuinely concerned that you may become homeless? No, right? So what's "enough" money? Go to India! See how wealthy you are.

"My body is too big."

Is that a fact?

Too big for what? For whom? Can you not make it through the door? Are you incapacitated? Are you in pain? Is your doctor concerned that you're taking years off your life? Are scientists coming to your house to evaluate you as part of a study of body-bigness?

"There are no men out there."

Is that a fact?

Um, when was the last time you went to a sports bar on game day? It's a sausage fest. And there are twelve dozen different kinds of single guys out there! Have you been to an art museum on a members' night or to a wine tasting Meetup, or checked out Bumble or another app? Single men are everywhere. Are you looking for a man you *think* you should be with or one you might actually be happy to be with, one who doesn't have to match the fixed idea in your mind?

Then we can go a little deeper. Can you stamp this thought with a 100 percent *fact* wax seal? What if what you've been thinking and believing about yourself — even for your whole life — *was simply a wonky theory*? What if it's — gasp! — just a hypothesis? The opposite of a fact is not fiction. It's simply a theory. And do you know what a theory is when you don't have all the accurate information in place? It's a *conspiracy theory*. Yep. You might have been conspiring against yourself way longer than you even know.

You can see this more easily when observing other people.

For example, you might know siblings who have very different ideas about what their childhood was like. Or you might meet someone who has an odd idea (to you) about how they look. They might criticize tiny things like the lines around their eyes or a birthmark they hate, but all you see is gorgeous. Maybe you'll be in an office environment where one person will thrive and relish their hardworking colleagues, while another will call it toxic and complain at every meeting about something (yawn).

Once at a wedding that Heath and I went to, some other women and I were gushing in the bathroom about the big white flowers, the live band (Aretha Franklin covers? *Yes, please!*), and the beautiful sunset. I was thrilled for my friend Lauren, the bride, who had pulled it all together and who was blessed with spectacular weather to boot. I particularly thought the luge was cool, and I was the first person to try it.

Walking past the luge after leaving the bathroom, high on our shared excitement, I heard another woman bark, "An ice sculpture? With vodka? How tacky."

So.

What's a fact here?

Nothing, really.

Just one important thing — *what you decide to make a fact in your own head.*

Here's how I used the fact-finding method with a client on a stuck belief that was making her feel despondent and frustrated:

"Everyone is more successful than me."

Is that a fact?

"Well, not everyone, exactly. But some people are. They are younger than me and they own more real estate and they have more money."

Okay. Is it 100 percent factual that "everyone" is more successful than you?

"Um, no, I guess."

How does this fake fact serve you then, exactly?

"It doesn't. It makes me sad. Desperate. Frustrated. Stuck. In a manic panic and rush…but toward what, I don't know."

Imagine that we extracted this fake fact from your mind, put it in a bubble, and then blew it away?

"Oh, man. I'd be really calm. And probably more creatively free than ever."

Do you see how her hypothesis here — that she is behind in life — repeated over and over again and therefore becoming forged into a belief, was ruining her peace? And it's only a theory! A theory, unproven and untrue, was making her miserable. What's funnier and more freeing than that? I'm not kidding — this exercise has me in hysterics with clients sometimes, over theories ranging from "my stepkids hate me" to "my boss has it in for me."

When we turn it all around, the absurdity of it shows up as laughter much of the time. Seeing events and people through a lighter lens helps us laugh instead of despair. We can wave away the nonsense that upsets us instead of choosing to be offended and being so damn serious all the time. Because no matter what happens, it's all temporary anyway. All of it. The house you live in. The watch you're wearing. Heck, even the person you're married to. We're all going to be dust one day.

Stress cuts us off from joy, creativity, and sound decision making. Levity brings clarity. When we're bogged down and heavy, is that the best time to make a big life call on something? Heck, no. What about when we're lighter, clearer, freer of mind? Probably. The shortcut to this wiser frame of mind can almost always be found in humor.

DIRECT MESSAGE

When you're feeling light and happy, even laughing about something, think about a perceived problem for a second. Do you see it differently? I bet you do. This is the lens that's not fogged up with theory. It's the real you. And doesn't the real you feel good?

I recently read an article in *People* magazine about a thirty-five-year-old woman who wrote her own obituary before dying of cancer. "Thirty-five years may not seem long, but damn, it was good!" wrote Bailey Jean Matheson.

What else did she say? "Don't take the small stuff so seriously."

And most of it *is* small stuff, when we think about it. Because not laughing enough is no joke!

Check this:

☐ Use a picture of a skull or a cemetery as your phone screensaver for a week. Trust me on this! (Let it freak people out.)

☐ Take a couple of minutes and write down what feels serious in your life right now. Maybe it's:

- money worries?
- job security?
- health issues?
- an unhappy marriage?
- a disagreement with a friend?

Let it all out. Don't hold back! This in itself can lighten the serious-seeming load on your shoulders. Freewrite for as long as you need.

☐ Take a few deep breaths, and notice how you feel now that all your serious worries are on paper. They might look more real on paper. But they also probably look less scary.

☐ And then — without any pressure — consider this question: *Is this a fact or a theory?*

CHAPTER EIGHT

Second Opinions Aren't Better Than Your First Feeling

Practice listening to your intuition, your inner voice;
ask questions; be curious; see what you see; hear what you hear;
and then act upon what you know to be true.
These intuitive powers were given to your soul at birth.

CLARISSA PINKOLA ESTÉS, *Women Who Run with the Wolves*

I'll never forget a sweet email I received from a former colleague when she read a *Marie Claire* article I'd shared on
LinkedIn. "I had no idea you could write! Wow, Susie. You're so
good at advertising sales, who knew you could do this whole
other thing, too?"

*I knew. And if I never acted on what called me forward, no
one else would ever know, either.*

From your career choice to the decision to have a family
(or not), to where you live...you *know*. And you can decide to
start knowing in any second, no matter how far you've pushed
your intuition outta the picture. It's silently there — always on
demand.

Consider this lighter example. If you were looking to take

a warm winter vacation to Cabo, Mexico (where you'd always wanted to go), and had a pleasant vision for your getaway, then it's the right thing for you. That's the place to go!

But what if you asked around? Crowdsourced ideas on where your vacation should be? Got opinions from online commenters, your parents, your colleagues? You might end up skiing in Colorado — pissed off and freezing. You'd be dreaming of a quiet hammock at sunset but instead your fingers will have stuck to a chair lift because Kelly (the alpha in your friendship group) said it's "the place to be" in February. And what does Kelly know? What's right for her! Nothing wrong with that. You asked. But maybe you forgot to remember — *you're not Kelly*.

This is a great example of the confirmation bias — our tendency to cherry-pick information that confirms our existing beliefs or ideas. Kelly's gone skiing in Colorado and liked it, so that's her version of the best thing to do. And if you let assertive Kelly keep going, she'd probably tell you which airline to fly, where to stay, and what to eat...and to def skip out on the overrated Irish coffee special (but you like whiskey with coffee, right?). Sad face.

But again, you're not Kelly. And you're not your parents, your older brother, Chrissy Teigen, or anyone else you might look up to. So how can anyone know what desires stir within you? They can't. Only you can. And your instincts, impulses, and intuition are 100 percent singular. So why discount them so rapidly? This is how we let so much misery enter our lives. Bronnie Ware, in her bestselling book *The Top Five Regrets of the Dying*, said the number one regret voiced by people on their deathbeds is, "I wish I'd had the courage to live a life true to myself, not the life others expected of me."

No matter how well-intentioned other people may be, they are not you. Your life is yours. You come into this world alone, and you leave it alone. Alone — you're equipped! You have the goods! It's all in there!

The Wisdom of Your Intuition

Your intuition is the inner pressing of the wiser you. It's the still, small voice inside giving you direction. It's the oldest, wisest part of you. Notice how every time someone gives you vacation recos, they'll describe the best activities based on what *they* did. Their intentions are good, and suggestions are wonderful if you're feeling them! But sometimes the pressure to "do all the things" in a new city is exhausting. You end up needing a holiday from your holiday. So if you got to Rome and you don't really feel like seeing the Vatican, the Colosseum, or that "must-visit" gelato bar...don't! *So what?* If you'd rather just drink Sangiovese, shop, eat pasta, and take in the atmosphere, then do that! It's *your* holiday. And it belongs to you. The same goes for choosing a career, a city, even a couch.

DIRECT MESSAGE

Say it with me: *my life is mine.*

Think of a time when you've trusted your intuition, even though it seemed to make no sense at all. What happened? Think of a time when you went *against* your intuition, because it didn't seem sensible to follow it. What happened?

When Heath was asked by his company to transfer to New York City from Sydney, Australia, at age twenty-three (I was twenty-five), some people thought it was too soon. And those concerns were well-meaning! I mean, we'd just moved into a nice, new apartment that we'd bought in Sydney. I had no job-transfer opportunity. Heath was still completing his college degree part-time at night school (and was only halfway through it), and moving was going to hugely complicate that. My job was safe there, and we had a nice life with his family close by. We heard things like:

> "New York will always be there, and it's so expensive. Save some more money and build your wealth here."
>
> "Heath should finish his degree and then see what opportunities there are. It's a rush and too soon."
>
> "You don't have a job lined up, that's pretty risky *cough* [read: reckless]."

But it was a 100 percent yes from both of us the second Heath's boss called him to make him the (frankly pretty underpaid!) offer. And moving to New York has been the best thing we've ever done, ever. Sure, it wasn't easy, there were arguments, and we even went to couples therapy a few times to address them, but all the issues eventually smoothed themselves out. And:

Heath found a way to finish his degree through another university that would send his exam papers to a testing center based in New York.

I eventually found a job, and within five years, at age thirty, I was making more than five times the amount of money I had been making in Sydney.

We managed to rent out the apartment we'd bought and hold on to it for a few more years before selling it at a nice profit.

The opportunities the move to NYC has provided us have been truly abundant and humbling. It all worked out! *Just say yes — you'll make it work.* That's what my intuition said. Look at any person you admire. If you listen to their interviews, read their biographies, or hear them on podcasts, you'll almost always hear something along the lines of, "I just knew I had to pursue this" or "Even though no one else understood it, I knew" or "Something inside me told me that this was my chance and I had to go for it."

DIRECT MESSAGE

Think for a second and take a deep breath. What is that knowing? That something inside? That voice?

It's your wise AF inner guidance. And no one else can tune in to it but you. It can help you with a million things — from choosing the right career path to meeting your life partner even to *saving your life*. Yep. It's that vital.

I was watching a documentary on the story of Colleen Stan, a teenager who was kidnapped while hitchhiking in the late 1970s. When some folks stopped to pick her up, she assumed that the couple, who had a baby with them, would be safe people for her to travel with. She reportedly "felt confident climbing into the blue van." When they stopped at a gas station along the way, she went to use the restroom.

"A voice told me to run and jump out a window and never look back," she recalled. But she ignored the voice, and she was taken to an isolated spot, held at knife point, and kidnapped. The couple held her captive as their "slave," keeping her in a coffin-size box, and tortured her for seven years. The case become known countrywide as "the girl in the box." Was a young couple with a baby a logical hitchhiking choice for a young girl? Probably. At least on the surface, they seemed a safe bet. Woman present. Little baby. Check! They're safe.

But what can the brain alone *not* decipher? Everything else. Only your instincts can — and Colleen Stan went against hers. If you had asked around the gas station that day, most people probably would have said "Yeah, they're a normal-looking family, a safe bet." Hitchhiking was common back then. But other people's opinions and learned behaviors are *not enough* for you to know the right thing for you.

Don't get me wrong, I'm not in any way blaming Colleen Stan for what happened to her that day. She was a young woman who was the victim of a kidnapping and was tortured by sick people. I have nothing but extreme sympathy for her. While I know this is a dramatic story in regards to making this point, it perfectly highlights something I think is very important: *we need, more than anything, to listen to the voice inside us that only we can hear.* Colleen didn't listen to her internal, guiding voice. Perhaps a second, less intuitive voice — the voice of the "they" — told her it would be impolite to run. Many of us, especially women, are taught to fight our instincts in this way. To tamp down our internal voices to make other people comfortable. And we must not do that. It can only lead us further from our own needs and desires, and as this case highlights, it can be very dangerous.

You've got to listen to your inner guidance.

Your Inner Pilot

Sara Blakely, founder of SPANX (and at one point the world's youngest self-made female billionaire — no big deal), is constantly talking about trusting her intuition. When I interviewed her for *Marie Claire* in 2014, she told me about the importance of spending time alone and really connecting with her inner guidance.

She said, "When you spend time alone, that's when your gut really has a clear channel to you. It's so important to trust it. I think that trusting your gut is like a muscle. The more you do it, the stronger it gets."

Hear that? *Alone.* Not with your three best girlfriends over brunch or your parents over dinner. You. *Just you.* You have the answers. And your brain alone isn't enough to come up with the answers. I think of the brain as a filtering system to assist you in confirming what you already know in your gut. It cannot be the sole decider, though.

You can listen to advice, yes. You can talk things out with people you trust. But only *you* can ever ultimately know what's best for you at any moment. The question you want to ask yourself is, *In this moment, am I letting my intuition guide me?* No one knows what's inside you, the same way that you don't know what's inside others. Your desires, intentions, and instincts are not felt by anyone but you. You have an inner pilot ready to drive your beautifully unique life forward…you just have to use it. It's your greatest treasure.

I've used my intuition in evaluating friendships. I had a good friend in Sydney named Maggie who I spent almost every weekend with when I was married the first time. We were close, our lives were similar and in sync, and I adored her. But after I separated from my husband and moved into my very small bachelorette pad, things changed. I started to have this weird dread when it came to seeing her. I always wanted to cancel on her for no reason that I could explain, and I'd feel anxious about our get-togethers. My brain didn't understand it. I mean, we were friends, right? What was wrong with me?

I was trying to adjust to my new life on my own, and I just didn't feel her support. It wasn't anything tangible. She certainly never said or did anything unkind (to my face). But then a mutual friend, Cameron, told me what she was saying about me behind my back: "Susie thinks she's such an it-girl. She's always out on the town because she can't be alone for five minutes."

Cameron responded by saying, "Hey, what if she knew you were saying this, Maggie?" To which she responded, "Whatever!"

When Cameron told me this, I wasn't surprised. It was confirmation of something I was feeling — that my life change had unsettled our familiar flow of things (change often does that). And Maggie wasn't okay with it. At a time in my life when I felt lonely and afraid and was just trying to get through each day as the only young divorced person I knew, she was saying mean stuff about me. Her words hurt. But I knew I wouldn't be able to change her thoughts or behavior, and to me, that was it for our friendship. It wasn't worth confronting her.

My "weird feeling" was right. I cut her out — and didn't miss her. We never even had a conversation about it. That was it.

Does cutting someone out of your life seem harsh? Maybe some would see it that way. But there's no guidebook to how anyone should live. There's no right or wrong way to experience a life, and you don't have to surround yourself with people who make you feel anything less than comfortable, safe, and supported.

Living a Self-Directed Life

Can you stop second-guessing yourself? Even the most extraordinary among us, those we look to for guidance, have ordinary problems just like we do. Other people don't know better, even though it can seem that way sometimes. And they certainly don't know best when it comes to knowing what's right for you. I'll never forget the time I heard a well-known spiritual teacher say onstage, "I've written six self-help books and I'm a f*cking mess!"

This is where self-approval will save you a thousand times. When you can rely on your inner *like* button, you'll be living a self-directed life. And unlike all those people on their death-beds wishing they'd lived a life truer to themselves, you'll reach that stage with far fewer regrets. And the sooner you can get there, the better for you. You don't have to wait until you're on your deathbed!

DIRECT MESSAGE

I knew my divorce was inevitable a year or so before it happened. I think my husband and I both knew. But denial is a very alluring place to live. The day we agreed to separate, I called my husband from the small, dark stationery cupboard at work (it was the only private space in a very open office). My inner voice couldn't wait a single second longer. We didn't say much. Just, "Hey, I love you, but this can't go on, right? Okay. Yep. I'll look for a new place."

That was it. A defining moment in a sixty-second conversation sitting on a box of Post-it notes. Intuition doesn't need candles, mantras, or a second opinion. It just needs you to listen.

When you trust yourself, not only will you make better, aligned decisions, but you'll have far more fun, too. Your inner guidance doesn't just want to keep you safe. It wants you to have a rich, full, healthy, vibrant, playful life! Because the basis of a good life is joy, freedom, and personal progress. That is what the universe is always supporting. And using your brain, tradition, or societal rules alone can hinder that.

One January morning, when my regular yoga class became a mat-to-mat experience, I had to laugh a little at the universal New Year's enthusiasm. But in this particular class, the teacher said something cool to all the newbies in the room: "If you lose your balance and fall, that's perfect. If you don't know the pose and have never heard Sanskrit before, that's perfect, too. Just copy the rest of us and try your best. If you're confused and regret coming at any time — also perfect! Just enjoy yourself. Explore your body's limits. Play around."

And as the class kicked off, I was surprised by something: the experienced yogis seemed to have the least fun of all. I noticed their furrowed brows, their discomfort when toppling during a standing balance, and their rushing ahead instead of flowing with the breath.

As for the newbies, one of them asked, "Hey, what's an asana?" They were just throwing themselves in wholeheartedly, and it didn't matter that they didn't know the terminology. They had the *most fun*, and probably got the best workout, too. A couple of them even went for it with headstands — something I never even attempt after nearly ten years of going to classes! And it worked, dammit!

Again, take a breath and think of a time when that brain of yours entirely led the way. What happened?

Now take another breath and think of a time when your heart led you fully. What happened?

Reflecting on that for a moment, do you want more of those heart-driven, intuitive moments to create your life? Probably, right?

There's nothing wrong with using your head. It's an amazing decision-making filter that keeps you safe and helps you make sound decisions. But the brain isn't pro-experimentation. It's not willing to look stupid, take a risk, or make a mistake. Our heads like routine and the perceived security it brings us. But not every decision needs to be sensible. Pure sensibleness blocks opportunity. The universe gave us a brain *and* a heart. We need to use both in making decisions.

So what's the heart like as a guide? Well, it doesn't overthink. It feels. It goes where it's called. And who knows where that can take you? Maybe something as unexpected as a successful headstand (that would've taken your brain more than a decade to arrive at).

Instant Intuition

If you're still feeling stuck, here's a potent Instant Intuition technique that will help you make the right decision:

Sit down comfortably.

Take a few deep breaths to clear your mind and settle the body.

Close your eyes.

Visualize your first option. See yourself moving forward with this choice. Picture it happening in the present moment in vivid color. Imagine the activity, the outcome, the ripple effects.

Keep breathing, and notice how your body feels and responds.

Now visualize your second option. See yourself moving forward with this choice. Picture it happening in the present moment in vivid color. Imagine the activity, the outcome, the ripple effects.

Keep breathing, and notice how your body feels and responds.

If there's a third and fourth option, keep going until you've covered them all.

Which option made your body relax? *That's the best decision for you.*

See? Your body will support you in making the right choices. Your body houses around 30 to 40 trillion of the most intelligent cells on earth! Respect them!

Anything that creates a spark of curiosity within us or generates some desire that typically lies dormant is often our intuition guiding us to say yes to more. Human beings are different from all other animals. We have the gift of higher consciousness and the ability to make choices using both our instincts and our intellect. We have this wildly helpful thing called instinct, *and* a brain that's smarter than any computer that exists. We can feel *and* think. We can understand doubt, process it, and use our intellect to reason. And when you use everything that's available to you, you'll never have to blame anyone else again. You realize how powerful you are in creating your life. And you won't let yourself down.

Check this:

❏ Say it aloud often: *my life is mine.*
❏ Think of a time when you've trusted your intuition, even though it seemed to make no sense at all. What happened? Write it down.

❑ Think of a time when you went *against* your intuition, because it didn't seem sensible to follow it. What happened? Write it down.

❑ When faced with your next big decision, ask yourself, *In this moment, am I letting my intuition guide me?* Be still and listen.

❑ Let the wise cells in your body help guide you. Use the Instant Intuition technique anytime you need it.

CHAPTER NINE

Ask, "What's Missing?"

*Sometimes you just don't know what's missing
until it arrives.*

ANONYMOUS

When I was a kid, I lived in a rural county in the United Kingdom called Cornwall. The only industry it had was farming, and lots of my friends lived on or near their parents' farms. I used to shake my head at how unglam my hood was when I had to stop the car to let sheep cross the road.

The UK's relationship with Europe was different back then — the European Union was smaller — and so my little county was considered one of the poorest regions within the United Kingdom's and Europe's borders. The government was concerned that kids in my region were missing school to support their friends and families because of the small, vulnerable farming industry.

Anyway, Brussels (the headquarters of the EU) declared

that Cornwall had what was called Objective One Status. This meant we got government aid simply so we could go to school. Yep. Thirty British pounds a week (around $38) if your household income was below a certain threshold or if, like mine, your family was on welfare. We teenagers couldn't believe our luck! (We were too naive back then to understand how serious it was for some people — too distracted with *yay, new jeans!*)

One day we had class with our cheerful geography teacher, Mrs. Davis (who I had no idea was a farmer's wife, too). She explained that because of international trade agreements, we had "milk lakes and butter mountains"— meaning that farmers were producing a surplus that couldn't be used. The irony! Starving children in the world and these "mountains" of dairy products going to waste. It was a political problem, she explained.

Then Mrs. Davis showed us a news segment. It showed large farms that looked almost closed across the UK because farmers were being paid *not* to produce. They got a subsidy for doing nothing because the overproduction was becoming a problem.

What do you think those farmers were doing?

Taking a well-earned break? Going on vacation? Enjoying daytime TV? Some might have been. But there was a far bigger problem, and it was about more than the crops and the dairy. It was that the pride, purpose, and joy in running farms that had been in some families for generations was being taken from them for an indefinite amount of time.

And the farmers were killing themselves.

Their reason for getting up every day was gone. Their purpose and identity had been taken from them, and they didn't know when (or if) it was coming back. It was tragic. It highlighted to me the unfairness of the systems we all lived under.

But it also made one other thing clear: *work is not just about the money*.

Yes, we need money. A decent, fair amount of it, too. It's a sad thing to spend a lot of time and energy over money worries (I knew that from the earliest age). But money itself is not enough. You'd think that being paid to do nothing would be a win, right? But it was the opposite. Most people wouldn't want that for long. It's not why we're here. These farmers' bills were being paid, sure, but something critical was missing. The "why" of getting up every morning.

Given where I grew up, I've met many farmers over the years and I've always found them to be extremely hardworking. I know they work from dawn till dusk, and they speak with such pride about their animals and their land. "I've the best office in the world — wouldn't trade it for nothin'," my dad's pal said once over a pint of lager at a local pub. Farmers' love of their work is palpable, and you couldn't imagine them doing anything else.

Deconstructing Dissatisfaction

It was an important lesson that I learned young: if you don't love your work, your contribution, something will always be missing.

Missing. It's a good word. Too often, our brains skip over the idea that something is missing and just recognize something as being plain wrong instead. This keeps us stuck — and often in despair. As a result, "What's missing?" is one of my favorite coaching questions to ask almost anyone.

Once I was coaching a lawyer named Elle who made great money and who seemed to have a nice family and a great life overall. She told me she was on antidepressants and couldn't figure out why she felt so dissatisfied. Everything was "good enough," so she felt guilty about her lack of joy. I asked, as most therapists and coaches would, "Well, what feels wrong? Or off? When did this all begin?"

DIRECT MESSAGE

In some cases, we simply can't pinpoint what's wrong. It can be a confluence of small things that build up over time. And so a different question that's great to ask is, "What's missing *right now?*"

When a doctor can't identify an illness, they often will classify it as stress or depression. And then we leave the doctor's office with prescriptions for drugs we don't necessarily want or that aren't genuinely a good fit for us. When I hear about this, it often reminds me of the words of the late dancer and musician Gabrielle Roth: "In many shamanic societies, if you came to a medicine person complaining of being disheartened, dispirited, or depressed, they would ask one of four questions:

- When did you stop dancing?
- When did you stop singing?
- When did you stop being enchanted by stories?
- When did you stop being comforted by the sweet territory of silence?"

For my client Elle, *friends* were missing. As part of the sandwich generation — taking care of her aging parents and her kids plus holding down a demanding job — she rarely saw her friends. Seeing friends regularly is a proven way to boost our spirits, lower cortisol, and even ease hypertension.

Just making the effort to reconnect with her girlfriends over sushi (or even a forty-five-minute glass of wine after work when that's all she could squeeze into the calendar) lifted her up so much that her husband now encourages her to do it regularly. He sees a marked difference in her when she spends time with the women she loves. "They bring her back to herself," he says.

That Missing Piece

On the path to satisfying your deep, personal desires — when things go wrong or feel off (and they will) — you can always ask, not what's wrong, but *what's missing*. I read this statement a long time ago, and it's stuck with me ever since because it applies to nearly every problem.

When we think about what's wrong, we panic. When we think about what's missing, however, we become creative! It opens us up. We don't have a stress response but a loving, open, innovative, even *inventive* response.

It's a question that addresses the same issues — but with way more success. Do you see the giant distinction here? When my mom was fifty-five, she went to college to earn her diploma in childhood education. She had been a math teacher in Poland before she moved to England, and she missed working with children. But with English as her second language, and a strong Polish accent, she wasn't confident enough to be a teacher in a new country. The woman earned a master's degree from the University of Warsaw, which was almost impossible, especially for a woman, during the Communist regime after Hitler's war.

After the years passed and her five daughters grew up, she

went back to school. In an earlier chapter, I mentioned that these days, in her late seventies, she still works as a volunteer three days a week at a local school, where they call her Granny. But I didn't mention that to get there, she had to get a whole new diploma in England in order to start working again and do what she loves. She encouraged the younger teachers, and as a woman living on her own, she cherished the connection to the community her job gave her, as well as the great contentment.

I respect this woman so much for *knowing what was missing* and having the courage — at age fifty-five — to join a classroom full of women less than half her age so she could pursue what she really wanted. She addressed what was missing. And it's been paying off ever since.

When I felt down for a period in my adult life, I forgot to ask myself this question. I kept thinking instead, *What's wrong with me?* I'd sit in my office during conference calls, gazing out the window at the New York City skyscrapers, and I'd constantly think, *Is this all there is?* The big buildings all around me felt like they were making it all worse — a ruthless reminder of other people's manifestation of their big dreams, while I was listening to cheesy jazz on-hold music waiting for someone who was late (again).

One morning when I was at my corporate job in one of my on-rotation pencil skirts, I was sitting in my freezing office. Doused in artificial light as usual, I numbed my boredom by scouring Pinterest. I saw a pin that struck me, a quote from Mary Oliver: "Tell me, what is it you plan to do with your one wild and precious life?"

"Not this!" my soul screamed.

It was time to fill the hole left by what was missing. Deep down, I knew. I loved to write, and I loved to help other people work out their personal problems. These two skills came naturally to me, but these parts of myself were not active in my job at all. And so it began: my side hustle as a life coach and writer. It marked the true start of the rest of my life. There was a gaping hole in making what's become my life's work a reality, and I had to fill it. Overnight, after I signed up for life coaching classes at New York University, *I felt different.* Let's not overthink this. What's missing can be found. It's willing and waiting and wanting to be found. And fast. But no one else can help you harness your inner desires, because no one can feel them but you.

Remembering that you don't need anyone else's approval (and that no one else knows what they're doing either!), answer this one question:

What's missing, my friend?

So you don't love your career — what's missing?

So your relationship's in a rut — what's missing?

So you want to be closer with your distant sibling — what's missing?

So you don't feel energized most days — what's missing?

So you feel life is passing you by versus really being *lived* by you — what's missing?

I want to stress that this doesn't have to be super serious or significant. You don't have to start a side hustle or a charity, or save the world. As with Elle, the solution can be as simple as one night out a week with a pal.

For a six-year-old girl I used to babysit when I was on a gap year in Sydney, the missing piece was a different kind of appreciation. I was sitting with her outside her violin teacher's room one day, waiting for her private lesson to start. Ting would sit quietly, holding her violin case, swaying her feet, which didn't touch the floor. I admired her perfect braids and calm, focused energy. I also took her to Mandarin, theater, and ballet classes. The girl's life was privileged, sure. It was also less flexible than an inmate's in a maximum-security prison.

"Ting, you're so well behaved," I'd tell her almost every time we saw each other. Her uncomplaining nature and obedience were unrivaled.

"Thank you," she'd answer, looking straight ahead.

This day before violin practice, she said, "Everyone says 'Ting, you're so well behaved. Ting, you're so smart. No one ever says, *Ting, you're pretty.*'"

My heart nearly burst for this little soul. Beneath her busyness and academic wins, she was a regular girl, just like me. Just like all of us.

"You *are* beautiful, Ting!" I exclaimed as the violin teacher opened the door. Ting walked straight into the big, mahogany room without looking back. I felt a twinge of sadness as I saw her teeny backpack bop away from me. Then the door shut with a thud.

I hope she heard me.

What's missing can be something you needed to hear as a child, which then becomes what you need to nurture within yourself as an adult. More recently, I was at a women's retreat and was asking the ladies I was with, "What's one thing you like about yourself physically?"

I love to ask this question because no one else does in our self-critical culture. And I adore nothing more than some unabashed self-lovin'. The women — after some time — gave various answers: good hair, strong arms, big green eyes, cute feet. But one woman named Ashley struggled to say anything at all.

"I've never thought about it," she said.

"Well…shall we think about it now?" I asked. I didn't want to push her, but my instincts told me to encourage her.

Before we go on, let's get one thing straight: *all* women are beautiful. And Ashley had so many lovely features I could list! When I met her, my first impression was that she was striking. But at that moment she remained silent. After a while, she said, "My mom always told me I didn't get the 'good' Asian features. I've never felt like I'm *allowed* to like my looks."

She said it was an uncomfortable revelation. Our parents can do a number on us, right (see chapter 1!)? But ultimately, when we figure out the ways in which a parent has prevented us from accepting ourselves, we can start on that good, healthy, self-love path. And that's a great moment. Because the time to start liking (and loving!) yourself is today. What are you waiting for? Is there something you are waiting to hear?

There's no better time than the present moment to consider what missing ingredient could contribute to your happiness. Want to identify what might be missing for you? Let's do it!

"What's Missing for Me?"

This "What's Missing for Me?" exercise should come with a warning sign because it might just solve a lot of your problems. Write down five to ten things that you:

- Never said aloud that you wanted
- Felt sad about never receiving
- Never told anyone else about
- Never gave yourself freedom to dream of and plan for
- Never allowed yourself to make real
- Never asked for

Keep asking yourself, "What else?" Don't be shy — this is just for your eyes! Once you've written down all the answers, take a few breaths. Then review your list.

What common theme appears? Is it more time alone, more ambitious goals, more adventure? As you reread your list, you'll probably see a few dots connect. The exact ideas you have might not be repetitive, but a deeper desire beneath them might become clear. For example, if your list looks like this:

- Travel to Tokyo and Kyoto
- Develop friendships with people who share my interest in long-distance biking
- Take a photography course
- Go hiking more
- Finally give online dating a shot

Then you're probably looking to get out of your comfy box, my friend. I know it's hard to begin, but consider this. If you're expanding that zone a little at a time, how big will your world become? Think of all the possibilities!

If your list looks more like:

- Find an hour to read a magazine and take a nap on the weekend
- Have more help at home — my to-do list never ends!
- Go for a long lunch with an old friend without feeling guilty
- Make time to get my hair trimmed more frequently
- Eat more healthily and make more time to cook

Then you might need to take better care of yourself. Guess what? You're allowed to do that. And you don't have to waste a single second feeling guilty about it, either. A well-rested, well-fueled human isn't better just for herself but for everyone around her, too. As the old saying goes, you can't give away what you don't have.

If it's:

- Call my brother (it's been a very long time)
- Meditate to be calmer
- Go to a seminar on spirituality to understand my anger better
- Ask someone I trust to help me convey what I mean more clearly at work (I sometimes get impatient and flustered)
- Try to find a relationship counselor who works for my partner and me

...Then you might need to work on some self-compassion and invest in creating a more peaceful you. What would it be like if you regularly felt more peaceful moments? How would life be different? If your desires don't seem to connect, don't worry — there may be lots of pieces waiting to be added to your life. And that's exciting!

But for now, start small.

Plan one thing this week that fills what's missing. Just one thing. Within seven days! Repeat it the following week. Remember, you only need your own approval here. And the person you need to satisfy and impress when it comes to doing this? It's you. Repeat. See what unfolds. And DM me on Instagram so I can enjoy it with you! @susie.moore.

Being in Harmony with Your Needs

Remember this truth: how you spend your days is a direct, honest reflection of your truest priorities. There are no exceptions to this.

Because finally taking that trip to France, making amends with a relative after years of conflict, or even enjoying a simple glass of Chardonnay with an uplifting friend on a Tuesday night might be the remedy that you need. And you want to be in harmony with your needs, not at war with them. Happiness cannot exist without harmony.

This truth showed up for me when I did something totally unexpected and out of my comfort zone: I went on a rock-climbing retreat.

Rock. Climbing.

I am *not* sporty. I'm like that meme you see floating around on Instagram: "I'm outdoorsy in that I like drinking on patios." But out of the blue, I felt called to do something new. And totally different. Maybe it's because I lived in New York City and craved nature. Or my body needed to be stretched. Or I wanted to meet a group of people who had nothing in common with me so I could remember how big the world really is. Whatever the reason, I saw the event advertised and without waffling for a second, I booked it.

DIRECT MESSAGE

Jon Acuff, author of *Finish*, says, "Be brave enough to be bad at something new." If you're willing, even the teeniest bit, to do something new and not be especially good at it and still have a good time, the world is yours.

The retreat welcome packet arrived, and it stated that I needed to bring a bunch of stuff I don't own, like a backpack, a flashlight, hiking boots, high-SPF sunscreen (yeah, I know I gotta get with the SPF, but it's hard for us Brits sometimes). I'll admit, I swung from, "This will be rad and *so* wild!" to "What the heck am I thinking? This was such a stupid impulse."

But I trusted that my initial enthusiasm and intuition were right. So I just threw together what I had and made it work. I embraced the adventure and felt good about it. I climbed a freakin' mountain! I didn't reach the summit, but who cares? It felt like a mini miracle to me. Despite feelings of doubt, there was one thought I kept coming back to as my mosquito bites itched like hell:

I'm proud of myself for doing something completely new, even though it felt uncomfortable, especially since I was the least experienced person in the group. Feeling discomfort is a sign that we should check in with ourselves. Sometimes being uncomfortable in a situation means we need to stop, but sometimes it's a sign that we're experiencing growing pains and that we just need to push forward! It's all about listening to ourselves and our bodies to figure out which is which.

I'm thrilled that I'm willing to be crappy at something. And that's where real confidence comes from. You don't clear your fear so that you can pursue new things. You pursue new things to clear your fear. *Read that again.* Because only action cures fear.

It's doing scary things that increases your self-esteem and self-assuredness. Not the other way around. No one ever became brave watching *Keeping Up with the Kardashians* on repeat (although I do dig that show on a lazy Sunday). You get brave by living your life and allowing discomfort to be a fair chunk of it. It makes life rich, too, don't you think? Doing something totally new and unfamiliar to you? It's like being a kid again.

Doing new, hard things, from launching a business to stretching your body physically, is even easier when you can ask yourself this question:

Where's the pressure for me to be perfect out of the gate at this new thing?

In. Your. Head.

I'm willing to be bad at rock-climbing, among other things — and have a blast nonetheless. Because it's no one's job to be good at everything. So you can resign from being perfect at *any* endeavor right now. Phew. You can relax! There's nothing to prove. Remember, life is to be enjoyed, not endured.

Think for a moment: What is something you're willing to be bad at? And why might that be good for you? Trying something new is good in and of itself, and while that particular thing may not be what's missing in your life (rock-climbing in particular wasn't necessarily missing from mine), it's the fact that you're trying something, stretching yourself, getting out of your comfort zone, and opening yourself up to *finding what's missing* that matters. And that's what doing something fun and new and challenging like going rock-climbing (if you're not normally someone who does that!) can bring to you. Right now I'm psyched to have more nature and physical beauty as a part of my world.

Whatever you decide to try, doing your best is enough. And don't let the world (or social media) fool you into thinking that fame, fortune, and the adoration of others is the answer to what's missing. If that were true, rich and famous people would never kill themselves, when sadly, suicide is more common among celebrities than it is among many other populations.

So let's relax into it, okay? This life thing is meant to be full and fun. The next time you don't feel great, or you feel plain restless, ask yourself the delicious, curious question: *What's missing?*

Think about it. Needy, unhappy, draining people rarely have questions. Because there's no curiosity there! That's not you. You have needs, yes, because you're a human, but you're not "needy" — because you don't just want to complain about your needs. You're curious and open and willing to satisfy them. That's why you're reading this book.

Remember, curiosity fuels wisdom. Even our sockless friend Albert Einstein said, "I have no special talents. I am only passionately curious."

There's no pressure. The answers will present themselves when they're met halfway with your willingness. Stop searching for a problem. When you search for problems, you'll find one (or several) just because our brains like finding answers. Do yourself the favor of a lifetime and locate what's *missing* instead. It's a fun space to be filled as opposed to something terrible to be fixed. Then see what happens!

Because the authority in your life always knows how to fill that space once you pass her the mic. So pick it up, will ya?

Check this:

❏ Complete the "What's Missing for Me?" exercise. Free-write!

❏ Keep asking yourself, "What else?" Keep going until you've written it all out.

❏ Take a few breaths, and review your list.

❏ Take action on one thing this week that's missing for you. And another the following. Journal on your emotions after taking the action and notice what arrives for you.

❏ Let it be fun (and easy).

CHAPTER TEN

Great News: It's Your Fault

Everything can be taken from a man but one thing: the last of the human freedoms — to choose one's attitude in any given set of circumstances, to choose one's own way.

VIKTOR FRANKL, *Man's Search for Meaning*

When I was around ten, I lived in what was probably my favorite women's shelter with my mom and sister. I'll never forget the time my mom's friend Mo came into our shelter with a bloodstained towel across her shoulders and my mom's arm wrapped around her. "Go to our room," my mom said.

That night, we went to sleep without my mom. She told us in the morning that Mo had gone back to her ex — who had attacked her, again. Because it wasn't enough that she already had a metal forearm. Yep, cut off at the elbow. She also had a clawlike thing for a hand (she used to joke with the kids that she was *Edwina Scissorhands*). Her husband, in a crazed attack, had mutilated her years before, which resulted in her losing her arm. And she still went back to him when he called.

Sadly, the more shelters we lived in and the more domestic violence I heard about, the more I understood how common it was for women to go back to their abusers.

Who needs horror movies? Reality is the most chilling of all.

We loved Mo. She was fun and nice and always let me eat her orange M&Ms (they taste a little different from the rest, if you've never noticed). I think she saw how rarely my mom got us candy, so she'd pick up a packet here and there when she got her Marlboro Lights. In a shelter where a lot of people come and go, Mo was a long-timer like us. And she felt like part of our family.

I should have felt desperately sad and worried for her, right?

But inside, I felt something else…

Fury.

What was she thinking? Why did she go back to him? She was safe with us! What the heck was wrong with Mo?

My sister and I probed my mom with these questions, and she always had the same answer: "It's her life. Her choice. There is no law against self-destruction." That last part was a statement she'd picked up in Al-Anon (a program of recovery for the families and friends of alcoholics) meetings, and I think this truism helped her be calm about some of the chaos in our own lives. "Plus, we don't understand mental illness properly," she explained. "We're only guessing."

As a kid, I wanted to shake Mo. *I'll never take any shit from men*, I promised myself. Now, as an adult, I understand that people stay with their abusers for a lot of reasons. My mom was right, in that there's a psychology behind it — some people grew up in abusive environments and internalize the idea that abuse is normal, or that they deserve it. Some are terrified to leave because they're worried they'll be harmed, or their kids will be harmed, if they do. Some are embarrassed to leave or feel ashamed. Some have debilitatingly low self-esteem, others are weighed down by their lack of resources. There are a ton of reasons people stay with or go back to their abusers. Some simply want to be loved and their abuser will tell them, "I love you."

I'm not trying to suggest that leaving an abusive situation is easy, or that it's the fault of the person who is abused that they have a hard time leaving. But eventually, they have to for their own survival. And if they have kids, for theirs, too. My mom was right — you can't just shake someone and knock them out of a cycle of abuse. But sometimes what someone needs to see their situation clearly is a person willing to tell the truth about what is happening.

You might be thinking, *How can being abused be someone's fault?* So here's my quick disclaimer: This chapter is not about victim shaming. It's not about making anyone feel bad for something terrible that happened to them that they had no control over. It's not about making people feel it's their fault that they got sick, were the recipient of racism/prejudice, were attacked, were born into poverty, or lost someone they love. It is about accepting your individual power and acknowledging that many of the unhealthy and toxic circumstances we find ourselves in are the results of us hurting ourselves. We sabotage ourselves much more than anyone else does. Sometimes we hurt ourselves directly, and sometimes we choose and use certain people to hurt us instead.

Don't Underestimate Your Competence

I had to shake myself for the first time as an adult around the age of twenty. I was making independent life choices at that stage, and so any blame for my mistakes was squarely on me. I moved to Sydney on a gap year between high school and college (a common thing for UK teenagers to do). I met a boy the second night after I arrived, and as you're now aware, we got married eight months later, on that beautiful Australian beach. *Wise, right? Get married at nineteen, kids!*

I hadn't been looking to get married at that age, but we wanted to stay together in one country, and marriage seemed like the only way to make it happen. It felt oddly practical. He was twenty-three and I was nineteen. I'd found a kind, caring, good-looking man, and that was positive, right? I thought I knew everything because I felt I had years of suffering already in the can. I thought I'd had my full portion of hard stuff already. But in just a short period of time, I realized that I knew nothing.

A few months into the marriage, I noticed "urgent" bills coming that weren't mine. Curiosity got the better of me, and I opened one. My husband owed thousands of dollars. I was floored. I didn't know how that could be possible. Because of my poor background and my horror at being wasteful, I went into a state of shock. Anger pulsed through me. *How could he have spent all that money?*

He was a gambler, and I had no clue. I missed all the warning signs out of innocence (and frankly, convenience — it's easy to shut out what we don't want to see). It slowly all became clear: the times my debit card was declined at the supermarket, the relatively new car that always seemed to need expensive repairs...The dread I felt, understanding that addiction can have a lifelong hold on a person, made me desperate. I knew recovery was possible. But I wasn't sure he wanted to pursue it.

Out of despair, I booked a meeting with a counselor. His name was Phil, and I called him Dr. Phil, like the TV host. I loved our sessions, sitting in the big comfy chair with the small hole in the armrest that I'd play with when Dr. Phil challenged my victim loop: "But I don't have family in this country! I need to stay! I can fix the issue here. He just needs my support!"

He'd say, "You came all the way to Australia on your own — you even paid for the passage yourself. You seem to have a nice career you're creating. Don't underestimate your competence."

Reread this last sentence: *Don't underestimate your competence.* Whatever statements you repeat to yourself, your mind will find reasons to back them up. Whatever you think repeatedly will attract more thoughts just like it. *That's how beliefs are formed.* The brain is our most powerful and obedient resource. Say it out loud:

"*I won't underestimate my competence.*"

Take some deep breaths.

Now we're a little more ready to tackle our victim loops. We all have them.

A victim loop occurs when someone has the same problem over and over and takes no responsibility for it or makes no plans to change it. The solution is to be accountable for the problem and apply action to solve it, what we call an "accountability loop."

Dr. Phil made one thing clear that I already knew but needed to remember: *what I'm not changing, I'm choosing.* Learning that I was stuck in a victim loop was the shake I needed to be awakened in that moment. Seeing my situation for what it was — a cycle of destructive behavior, fighting, gambling, lying, repeat — teleported me back to that night with Mo and my mom pressing a bloody towel across her shoulders. That memory, and its meaning in my life at that moment, stabbed me in the heart, the way that only truth can.

After my husband tried Gamblers Anonymous and never went back, I knew it was over. I was *not* going to live like any of those women I met growing up. No way, José. And so two and a half years after getting married, I moved out. It was terrifying. I had $1,700 in the bank, and my best friend lent me $1,000 for my deposit on the cheapest rental that she could help me find — all I could afford on my salary.

I loved my teeny safe haven. There was a massive burn mark (from what, I'll never know) on the carpet in the living room, and when you opened two of the kitchen drawers, they had no bottoms, just gaping holes. But I never complained about a thing because I was terrified the owner would try to raise the rent. The bathroom was a curious mix of dull pink and lime green. That part, weirdly, I kind of loved, too. And hey, I'd rocked far less in my life (another blessing in disguise from being a poor kid).

Most significant, it was *mine*. No one had keys except *me*. I practically felt like Carrie Bradshaw (sans the designer threads...but who needed those?). I had *my own place*! Some weeks, I had just Snickers, Red Bull, and some cheap prosecco in the fridge. *Freeeeeeeeedooooom!*

I had to get used to being on my own, which is a terrific life skill for anyone. Kitchen cupboard wobbly and a tad unhinged? Grab a screwdriver and tighten it up! Scared of spiders? Sleep with a can of bug spray next to your bed! And whatever you do, do *not* watch TV shows about ghosts or rapists.

A very human thing can happen when life "goes wrong," too.

People help.

It reminds us of the core of our humanity, I think, when we witness suffering or struggle. It binds us because it happens to us all. Maybe not in an identical way, but struggle is struggle, and it's obvious when we see it. In fact, it still makes me teary every time I remember something my best friend used to do for me back then. Alexis, knowing I was on a strict budget, used to drop by having "accidentally" overbought stuff (that she probably really stole from her parents' place) for herself: "Hey, I got too much Charmin/Dove/toilet cleaner at the supermarket. You may as well have it."

Her grace humbled me. When we hugged, I think she knew I knew. But we didn't say a word. Curiously, the day I left my husband, I never cried another tear over him. Not one. Boo-hoo, poor me. Sad, right? To be divorced so young? To be heartbroken and have my youthful idea of love shattered?

Wrong! I had decided to get married way too young, after knowing the man for just a few months. I didn't know the person I married. He's a good person but not my person. I grieved the marriage being over when I was still in it. I thought love was enough, but it's not. And I had to acknowledge that a huge chunk of it was my fault. Because it was my choice to marry someone after five minutes of knowing him. For choosing chemistry over compatibility. Who else is to blame here, exactly? *Cupid?*

I was young, yes. But I wasn't the five-year-old who broke a glass and shifted the blame to my sister, exclaiming, "Liz did it!" I was a grown-ass woman who *knew how to handle broken glass*. Right? When you admit your mistakes and clean up after them, it makes you brave. And — even though you don't know it in the moment — it reminds you that any future glass-breaking can also be met with your swift action. So don't cry for me, Argentina. This isn't the time for sympathy, it's the time for strength.

This truth made me feel oddly strong. And empowered. And able to make a better decision for myself next time. Accepting responsibility leads to enlightenment and the freedom not to repeat history. The second time around, I knew the right questions to ask early on; I knew how to find someone truly well-suited to me. How did I know how to make the great decision to marry the man who is now my husband? Because I accepted accountability for having been naive before.

Here's what I chose to accept, which helped me leave my victim loop for an accountability loop. Yes, my former husband's gambling was a problem, but I clearly had maturity issues of my own. Like the choice *I had made* in getting married so blindly (and so early), and all the subsequent choices I'd made to ignore the problem my husband clearly had. *My choices contributed just as much to the situation as his had.* Take that, victim loop! It like a painful, truthful "ouch" for a second, but then the relief of "Oh, yes, I'm powerful here" came immediately after. Accountability loops make you powerful. Victim loops, not so much.

Freedom = Responsibility

There's nothing so emboldening as taking responsibility for your choices, once you understand the autonomy it gives you. Author Wayne Dyer quoted Carl Jung as saying, "You are doomed to make choices." This is life's greatest paradox. Because choices equal opportunity. They equal freedom. But when the outcome isn't what we want? We don't always want the responsibility if it turns out badly, do we?

When a choice we make leads to a good outcome, we naturally want to celebrate our great decisions. But when one of our choices leads to something miserable, we want to distance ourselves from it. We don't want to acknowledge that what happened is a reflection of our choices. But when you pay attention, you realize that almost everything that's happened in your life is a result of choices you've made.

DIRECT MESSAGE

We make a lot of decisions unconsciously, so we tend to think we're not making choices all the time, but we are. Literally every action (and lack thereof) is a choice. And here's the deal: once we accept that outcomes, good or bad, are almost always the result of our choices, that frees us to take the next step with intentionality. Read that again. Being accountable for our decisions becomes an unexpected form of bliss. It means we've moved out of the past. And we get to decide what happens next.

I love to interchange "It's my choice" with "It's my fault." Sounds *disempowering*, right? It could. But not to me! "It's my fault" is the most powerful statement you can make when something bad happens that's within your control. And you're in way more control than you might realize, most of the time.

Why would you want to take the blame for something? Because if you don't, the price you pay is not being able to change a thing. Shifting blame to others gives every ounce of your power away. Here are a few examples of what this can sound like:

"She stole from me."

"But he betrayed me — I can't start over."

"I can't believe I got fired."

> "I don't know how there's so little in my savings ac-
>   count!"
> "I can't believe this is happening to me."
> "This is so unfair."
> "But he got the better client list."
> "My mom favored my sister, so now I comfort-eat."
> "No one encouraged me to get an education, and it's
>   too late now."
> "Life is just so stressful."

Do any of these sound like you? Be honest, now. Let's break these statements down, shall we?

"She stole from me." What did you make available in order for someone to be able to steal from you? Is this a lesson in being too trusting, perhaps?

"But he betrayed me — I can't start over." Betrayal happens. But when you think about it, that situation with the person who betrayed you is already in the past. You can choose to start over with someone else. And you can do it with any sunrise.

"I can't believe I got fired." Were there any warning sides leading up to being fired? The company not hitting sales targets, or a failed project maybe? Perhaps you'd checked out of your job mentally? Maybe it will make more sense once you honestly reflect on it for a moment.

"I don't know how there's so little in my savings account!" Money doesn't grow legs and walk outta your bank account. What have you been spending it on? Look at past credit card bills (I know it's hard).

"I can't believe this is happening to me." What is happening to you? Is it a fact or a theory? Consider the circumstances. Is it *truly* tragic? What part do you have control over?

"This is so unfair." Life is not meant to be fair. But it's still damn good! If life were fair, there would be a lot more people like you: with shelter, warmth, and safe, limitless drinking water; with access to books and literacy. Perspective helps when something feels unfair!

"But he got the better client list." In sales, when someone "got the better client list," it means they made more money. After years in sales, I realized that 80 percent of it was a talented seller turning a prospect into a good, lasting client — or retaining a high-maintenance client with a lotta TLC. There's no such thing as a good, fixed client list.

"My mom favored my sister, so now I comfort-eat." Your mom might have favored your sister. Have you talked this out with someone? But the past doesn't equal the present. While it can be difficult to get over past issues and traumas, you're a grown-up, and what you eat, do, and think is now entirely up to you.

"No one encouraged me to get an education, and it's too late now." It's never too late to get an education! Also...is education really necessary to achieve your goals? Look at all the success stories of people who never went to (or finished) college! Google it. It's a candy store of inspiration!

"Life is just so stressful." This idea is such a common, silent happiness thief. A woman I know is constantly trapped in this belief. She's launching a new project and (once again) feels stressed as hell. Her apartment move was stressful — fair enough. Then her relationship with her mother was making her crazy. Then she started sending me frantic-sounding texts for my biz advice on her various projects.

It's one thing to be stressed-out — heck, we all are at one time or another, right? But her stress is constant, and she thinks she relieves it by complaining to other people. Why isn't she accountable for this stress? Because she's stuck in a pattern of giving her power away. She doesn't consider that another person out there, perhaps with even more reason to stress out than she has, is just getting on with it. I want to shout, "There are innocent people imprisoned, dude!"

You don't have to live in a monastery to know that having fewer stressful thoughts is an option for you, no matter what. So on the days or phases of life when you find yourself complaining a lot (fess up — it can come in waves to us all!), you're very likely caught up in a bit of a victim loop.

Think for a moment: Where are you giving your power away? Is it to a person, a thing, a situation? We all do it. Maybe you find your work unfulfilling at the moment and you're bored with your job. So you say your boss is underutilizing you and doesn't see your value. These things may very well be true! But you also have control over whether to stay at that job, and you also choose whether to have a conversation with your boss about working on projects that are more fulfilling for you (more than once, if you have to). Who are you giving your power away to here? In this situation it's your boss.

And why is giving our power away so tempting? What's so helpful about shifting the blame, exactly? It feels like a *get out of jail free* card. And yes, you get a few minutes or days of sympathy texts and hugs when you announce something sad or unfair. But then what? Congrats! You're stuck with a crappy life that's happening "to you" rather than a life you're improving by choice.

And on that note of sympathy: it's so important that we don't mistake sympathy for love. Sympathy matters, especially when terrible, unpredictable things happen. But in many cases, we seek sympathy to soothe feelings of regret over choices we're not happy we've made. And that kinda sympathy runs out, fast. Sympathy can be a victim's version of receiving attention. A far better method of receiving legitimate love is through respect, and how do we receive respect and, most important, self-respect? Through being responsible for our lives.

Too often people get so caught up in the daily activities of life that they tend to just "go with the flow." And yes, it's important to be flexible, but when it comes to your life, you should be the one *setting* the flow. And hey, don't only dead fish go with the flow?

I spoke to a shy friend over breakfast about this once. She told me she was feeling miserable about attending a work conference where she wouldn't know a single soul. I told her, "Hey, you're not shy around me, your parents, your boyfriend…why act shy at conferences, clutching your phone for dear life at the back of the room?"

She didn't like the question because she felt safe in her *perceived-as-fixed* personality trait. She thought this trait was easier to live with than to question. But once we got curious and explored it, she came to see the value in the questioning. "We savor our misery like wine," said Ram Dass. We can relish our limitations when they seem to let us off the hook. But we also know that with some consciously applied self-approval, much can change, don't we?

And it matters. Because every lie we utter to ourselves puts us into a heavy-feeling, interest-accruing, personal debt to ourselves. And one day, you'll have to pay up. You can tell the truth to yourself now and take some action, or pay the price of regret later (more to come on shyness, too).

A friend of mine magnificently declined sympathy when she was diagnosed with type 1 diabetes. After speaking to doctors at length, Kim told me, "All I have to do is wear this bracelet and carry a little insulin pen around. It's not that bad!" Heck, what you can't change and aren't responsible for you can still choose to respond to in a pretty damn cool way. She even jokes that we shouldn't make her mad or she'll stab us with her pen. It's like she has no illness at all. In fact, she refuses to talk about her health pretty much altogether. As a result, almost no one even knows about it.

I can't help but contrast this with an old boss of mine, who had type 2 diabetes (which from my basic understanding is less serious and more manageable). She was constantly referencing her medical appointments and scary prognosis, and she always spoke in a foreboding way about her future. It's like these two women were talking about totally different conditions.

Here is the best news on earth: you are responsible for yourself and for your response to everything and anything at all. You can assert yourself and maintain an accountable attitude or reject your power altogether. Your life can be an accountability loop where you're in control or a victim loop where all power lies outside you.

Taking responsibility for yourself and knowing your own power won't prevent bad things from happening to you, but you'll be way better off when they do happen. Because they happen to us all. Your bounce-back rate from almost anything terrible will have people wanting whatever amazing drug they'll assume you must be taking.

As Glinda in *The Wizard of Oz* says, "You've always had the power." You have a palace within you. The key to it is in your hand. When you're accountable for your decisions, you're swimming laps in your luxury pool and deciding what to do all day. When you're not, you're slumming it outside, waiting for someone to give you instructions. I've come to realize that you never stop learning, and if you're living fully enough, you'll never stop lovingly shaking yourself into more accountability loops. There will never come a day when uncool things stop happening. And that's okay!

What You're Not Changing, You're Choosing

When I was thirty, I realized I couldn't trust my superiors at work. I was in a sales job, and when it comes to commissions, people can get *gree-ee-edy*. I had a manager who took credit for other people's wins, and I was stunned when I came to understand that all the "one team one dream" and "a win for one is a win for all" talk was just shiny corporate speak. In the final year I worked there, my boss swiped a fair amount of other salespeople's commissions (by firing them just before they were due a commission payment or by retroactively increasing their sales targets). I'm still incredulous thinking about it! But it was just another lesson in self-reliance.

I quit shortly after I realized what was going on. That experience helped me to realize that no one person, job, or career is the source of your good. And I knew the only way (for me) was to be self-employed. Because that felt right for me. But there are lots of options out there when it comes to jobs and literally every other aspect of your life. Are you choosing the right one, right now? Remember, *what you're not changing, you're choosing!* So don't give your options a cursory glance and call yourself stuck. I dare you to list three alternatives to any existing problem in your life. For example:

Problem: My husband doesn't respect me.

1. Go to counseling — work on it together.
2. Adjust your expectations of how respect should be demonstrated. What might you be overlooking? Maybe he's speaking a different love language. For example, maybe you want him to show his respect and affection for you by telling you certain things, but instead he shows his love for you by asking if he can pick anything up at the grocery store, and he always brings you coffee in the morning.
3. If the problem persists, leave him. Divorce is pretty common, if you haven't already noticed. Oh, and despite what anyone tells you, God cares about your joy and how you treat yourself and others more than your matrimonial paperwork.

Problem: My friends don't inspire me.

1. Take the initiative and join a local Meetup. Or try a new sport. Or take a new class. Or pretty much do anything where you'll meet new people. When you open your eyes, you'll find a million welcoming circles. Your new tribe can be anything you want it to be! As I mentioned earlier, rock-climbing opened my eyes to a whole new world. Now I have the coolest circle of sustainable-living-minded, strong, badass adventurers in my life. I

love it! But I had to take the scary step of climbing a steep-ass rock with them by signing up for a retreat.

2. Reach out to the positive friends in your periphery who are always posting optimistic messages on social media. You know who they are!

3. See your pals through an appreciative lens, and accept them as they are. If they're not a power posse, are they at least loyal, kind, supportive? No friend is perfect. What might you be overlooking? You can make new pals and honor the old!

Problem: I don't make enough money.

1. Ask for a raise or start a side hustle! (Check out my free workshop: sidehustleprepschool.com.)

2. Change jobs! Or if you're an entrepreneur, dial up your marketing efforts. How many more calls can you make and/or emails can you send a week? Add hustle hours to the calendar — twenty minutes a day, perhaps? Can you let job searching or marketing be a bit easier and a lot more fun?

3. If you can, move to a cheaper city or drop expensive habits like dinners out and unnecessary online shopping. Can you try a zero-dollar month, a zero-dollar week, or even just a zero-dollar day? Try to make a game of it. How can you be competitive with yourself and spend as little as possible? Consider the financial rewards you'll reap. It all adds up! Also, if you even track every outgoing dollar for a week, you'll see where it disappeared.

Problem: People take advantage of me.

1. Ask yourself, *What is it about me that makes this possible?* Is it your *disease to please*? Hey, I have it, too. That's okay. But I never say yes on impulse anymore. I wait twenty-four hours when I'm invited to something before I give an answer, and I have some firm boundary policies in place. (For instance, either Saturday or Sunday has to be a day with zero plans.)

2. If it's a particular person you feel takes advantage of you, can you limit interaction with him or her? It might be easier than you think to do this. Can you start lovingly saying no a little more often?

3. Have an honest conversation in which you lovingly convey what doesn't feel fair. Communication matters! You deserve to be heard and can start with something as simple as, "Hey, Jo, I really value our friendship. Because of that there's something I'd like to tell you about how I feel..." Using "I" statements makes the conversation feel less blame driven and more constructive.

Problem: I don't like my body.

1. Ask yourself, *What about it don't I love, and why?* What professionally Photoshopped images might I be comparing it to? Decide to like what you can't change. I embraced being short years ago. I've trained myself to love my petiteness.

2. If there's some aspect of your physical self that you think you can improve and are willing to, why not go for it? For instance, if you're balding and you don't

want to be, there are very effective treatments for that. Don't let any external voices tell you that you shouldn't make changes that *you* want to make.

3. Lessen the ego's hold on your physicality by focusing on nonphysical traits you like about yourself. Are you a great conversationalist? Have a great sense of humor? Make a mean crab cake? You get the picture. We're all getting older — one day that body you complain about will be in the dirt, so enjoy it while blood is pumping through it!

Saving Grace

Do you get the picture here?

Do you see the grace that can exist in reframing every perceived problem as being totally within your control? This section could come with a warning: *if you start to do this in every life area, not only will you experience far more freedom and elation, but people will start flocking to you.* Negativity, projected powerlessness, and cynicism repel people, no matter what or where.

Even unexpected delays that occur in day-to-day life can be relaxing, and when we see them in the right light, they become a chance to take on some long-awaited to-dos. And it's up to you to decide how you choose to perceive these delays. For instance, there's also a lot you can get done while waiting in a traffic jam, like:

- Listen to an audiobook.
- Check out an inspiring podcast (name-drop some of your faves!).
- Squeeze a hand grip.

- When it's truly bumper-to-bumper and you're not moving, do affirmations in the rearview mirror.
- Practice deep breathing.
- Set intentions for the day.

Here's an example of a situation I experienced that illustrated this for me:

Problem: A flight is delayed and it's horribly inconvenient.

1. Tweet the airline and see what they can do for you. (I've gotten so many bonus points this way!)
2. Shrug and get back to your Kindle.
3. Order a wine or a soda at an airport bar and call your mother.

Several years ago I was at an airport, waiting to go to Atlanta for a business meeting, and a flight delay was announced. One man lost his mind. He interrogated a crew member and huffed and puffed his way around the gate. I was surprised, because he was a sharply dressed, professional-looking man, and his lack of composure was a bit over-the-top.

There is one thing I knew for sure — everyone at the gate was secretly thinking, *I hope this bloke isn't sitting next to me on the flight.* Even though he was only rude to one person there, we all felt it. And we did not want any piece of it.

Negativity repels people, even when it's not directed at them (after this man's outburst, no one wanted anything to do with him). It also shows a lack of self-control. When you cruise the positive path, other people will often rise to meet you there. They'll want to be more like you.

Optimism isn't naive, it's a sign of leadership. Look around you. Who has the most friends, opportunities, and "good luck"? It's the positive peeps. Because they understand their power and use it, not abuse it. Actor RuPaul said, "Negativity is lazy," and he's right. When we use our power positively, the world opens up to us.

This doesn't mean that life is going to be a pure breeze. Because as you evolve, life's challenges remain. But you have the capacity to become more resilient with every knock. What's the alternative? If life's challenges stop, that means you're dead. And if you don't get stronger and recognize how much strength lies within you, you'll always be at the mercy of something. And having a FRAGILE label on your back is no way to live.

DIRECT MESSAGE

Have you ever heard the term *antifragile*? My friend Ron taught me it. It is a concept developed by Professor Nassim Nicholas Taleb in his book titled, well, *Antifragile*. It basically means that stressors, problems, and failures not only *do not* break you, but they make you strong. He says, "Antifragility is beyond resilience or robustness. The resilient resists shocks and stays the same; the antifragile gets better." Has this been true for you in some way? What's gone wrong in your past that has actually made you better, stronger, smarter somehow?

No matter how long a person, an incident, or a situation has been keeping you in a victim loop, consider that there are at least two good outcomes to any mistake. *Any* mistake. My divorce led me to make a far more mature decision in my second, lasting marriage. And it allowed me to live in beautiful Australia, where I also met Heath.

My untrustworthy boss helped give me the nudge I needed to go all in on my side hustle, which has since become the super successful business I secretly always wanted. It also made me a better coach and friend to people struggling with office politics.

I've learned another lesson along the way when it comes to any kind of abuse we tolerate from the people in our lives: what shows up in our lives *matches how we feel about ourselves*. How can it not? The world is always responding to our self-opinion. And when our self-opinion is shitty, we accept shitty treatment from others. Look around you! You'll see that this is true everywhere.

As a result, we only allow into our lives the level of abuse *we give ourselves*. If you want to understand how you feel about yourself, look at what's showing up in your life. I've never seen an exception. Your opinion of yourself will be matched over and over again.

Read that again.

The moment someone hurts you more than you hurt yourself in your own head is typically the moment you know that that person's time is up in your life.

In the various women's shelters I lived in, I observed that there was a moment when each woman had just had enough. It was the walk-out moment that led her to the shelter. My mom's first one was my dad's episode with the lighter and my six-month-old scalp. And that moment doesn't arrive lightly because it takes courage to walk into the unknown (often with no money or people to support you). The respect I have for these brave women — especially now, as an adult with a better understanding of the world — is immense.

My mom always told me that for every woman in a domestic violence shelter, there were a hundred more just like her too scared to leave. One woman said that her husband threatened to hurt their newborn baby. Another woman's husband told her that he'd drown her and tell her kids she abandoned them for another family. These were their walk-out moments.

So when is enough, enough? Well, that's up to you. Being in a bad relationship doesn't make you weak or stupid or anything else. It just meant you were willing to believe in something and someone. The mark of emotional health is *how long you put up with it once you realize how unhealthy it is and how unhappy you are.* This goes for anything — a toxic friend who gossips about you, receiving unequal pay at work, the passive-aggressive texts from your narcissistic sibling or parent. Don't buy it if someone tells you that you're being too sensitive if something feels wrong!

Because living a self-approved life means owning your choices and responses. Even, perhaps *especially*, the messy parts you may have been avoiding for a long time. Because what we're not changing, we're choosing. And living approval-free has to mean living blame- and excuse-free, too.

Check this:

- ❏ Understand that true freedom and power begin when we become 100 percent accountable for our lives.
- ❏ Get real with yourself for a moment and consider what victim loop you might be in. Ask yourself, *How can I*

turn this into an accountability loop instead? How can I take personal responsibility here?

❏ Take action on creating an accountability loop in a stuck/unpleasant area of your life. Have a difficult conversation, or set an exciting (even scary) personal goal.

❏ Repeat these statements to give you courage in standing up for yourself whenever you need to:

- *I will not underestimate my own competence.*
- *What I'm not changing, I'm choosing.*

CHAPTER ELEVEN

Fall Madly in Love with Rejection

Whatever happens around you, don't take it personally....
Nothing other people do is because of you.
It is because of themselves.

DON MIGUEL RUIZ, *The Four Agreements*

When I was eight, I wasn't invited to a pool party by a cool girl at school named Maria. I had a feeling it was because another girl at school had laughed and tossed aside the $1.99 stickers I'd given her as her present at her party the weekend before. Her other presents were Barbies and other cooler, more expensive toys. I liked the stickers (I mean, I even used to keep the *free* ones from cereal boxes all over my wall — and she dismissed the ones my mom had *paid for,* which were all we could afford)! *She's so mean. I wish I hadn't come,* I thought. The feeling of being rejected for not being good enough really stung. I still feel a twinge of sadness thinking about it now.

But I remembered something my mom always used to say,

along the lines of, "No one can make you feel bad — it's up to you." (I recognize it now as the famous Eleanor Roosevelt quote about feeling inferior: "No one can make you feel inferior without your consent.") When I related the story to my mom, she repeated that same quote again. And she didn't give me an ounce of sympathy. "Besides," she'd say, "being poor isn't a crime — being ashamed of it is." Her tough love on this oddly bolstered me up. Maybe it wasn't that bad.

> **DIRECT MESSAGE**
>
> Yep, it wasn't that bad. Tough love gives us perspective sometimes! A lot of sympathy isn't always what we need, whether we're kids or adults.

One of the greatest gifts my mom gave me as a kid was a love of reading, quotes, and wisdom. We'd read books of quotes, write uplifting ones down when we saw them, and talk about them. It made us all feel lighter. So I learned a lesson young: when things that are out of your control don't go your way, it's okay. Just *stop* wanting that outcome. Your emotions don't have to follow your observations. Your emotions can *lead* your observations. Because you are the only observer in your world.

How to Make Sour Grapes Sweet

I've always loved another of *Aesop's Fables*, from which we get the expression *sour grapes*. It's about a fox that can't reach the grapes on a tree. After many failed attempts, he walks away grapeless, saying to himself, "Well, those grapes were probably sour anyway." The moral of this story is that people criticize what they can't attain. We hate what we can't have. And this is too true. Anyone with critics — a smiley frenemy, a jealous coworker, online haters — understands this well.

But I think about this story a little differently: I've always liked the fox's attitude.

We don't always get the metaphorical grapes (the partner, the job opportunity, the coveted party invite, the long legs), and that's okay. But what if we could learn to detach from our desire for them with the fun help of a little shade rather than regretting their absence or loss?

Because negative thoughts will arise. You're probably fostering some long-held negative beliefs already about a few things (hey, it's okay, we all do). Maybe you wish you were as academic as your older sister. Or maybe a former college friend has been posting some perfect images of her glamorous business trips — and you're struggling to find a job. But instead of indulging these thoughts or distracting ourselves from them, we can *transform* them. I still call my sister when I need a sour-grapes talk. We used to do this when we were kids living in the shelters, crammed into one room. We'd say things like, "Dad's angry a lot. It's a good thing we don't see him very much." (We missed him a lot.)

We'd also say, "Yeah, the other kids at school have whole houses of their own, but we get to always be together in our room." (Of course, we were jealous of those kids, especially if they had pools.) It helped both of us to reframe the situation. It's insanity to rue when you can choose to let some relief in, right?! It's not about stuffing your true feelings down; it's about caring about yourself enough to let in some air and relief.

If you interview for a new position and don't get the job, you don't have to obsess over what you could have done differently or should/shouldn't have said in the interview. If you didn't get the job, *it wasn't your job*. Now think for a moment. What was the less-than-perfect truth about it, really?

Bad location? No work-from-home flexibility? A real bitch as a potential coworker? *You felt her attitude in interview number two!* Perhaps there wasn't that much of a boost to your paycheck or there was no signing bonus to celebrate with? Perhaps in your desperation to leave your current job, you thought that any other job would be better, but in the back of your mind you knew it wouldn't necessarily be. Sprinkle the negative lavishly. Let. It. Go.

Your pretty sister has had her own set of challenges, hasn't she? Maybe it was harder for her to be taken seriously in her job, or she got lazy because she could coast on her looks. And that college friend with all the kids? You may want the version of her family life she posts about on Instagram, but you definitely don't want the reality of the situation. You slept in this morning, whereas she probably spent the night mopping up vomit because one of her kids brought another bug home from school, and now she's back at it at 6:00 AM.

You can use this approach in any situation from super serious losses, like a spouse walking out on you (everyone who is divorced knows it doesn't happen overnight) to pretty minor stuff, like when the dry cleaner loses your blouse (hey, the color was fading anyway, wasn't it?). And using this technique is a lifesaver.

The sour-grapes lesson can be realized in even the worst

situations, even when the situation is traumatic and you wish you could unlive it.

Rejecting Rejection

During my years working in tech I was a suit-wearing, business-card-holding, briefcase-carrying (okay, maybe there was no literal briefcase, but you get the idea) saleswoman with scarily high New York City sales targets to reach. In that world, if you don't sell enough goods, you say goodbye to your job. And I was certainly not the seller with the most background in tech. I was definitely not the most connected, being new to the country. I wasn't even the person who stayed latest at the office or someone who is great on a team.

But two things worked in my favor:

1. I rejected rejection (I never even thought it was real, *because it's not* — more to come on that in a bit).
2. Stuff — like office politics — generally just didn't bother me that much (and I could never understand why people got so worked up over small things that took up all their energy).

As a result, I hit those targets just fine, and I was one of the most highly compensated salespeople in the company. I made a great living at a young age by using those strengths I identified early on: I'm good at asking questions, and I'm persuasive.

In some cases, I would try calling and emailing a potential client fifty-plus times to receive...silence. In other cases, people would be kinda rude and say, "We are *not* interested in any new partners. Please stop contacting us."

Hey, until I had a restraining order hit me in the face, I didn't care. I was just doing my job.

And to reiterate my fave question here, I thought, *So what? These people don't know me. I'm just a first name plus last name in their email in-box.* It would be absurd to take it personally. Ironically, it's the ego that feels hurt from being turned away. The *enlightened* part of you struts on. Because you know who you are! And it's not someone who whimpers when receiving a rejection note.

What made me so rejection-proof, exactly?

It was all those books and stories my mom and I would read: a lot of them included famous rejection stories. Like how Colonel Sanders's KFC recipes were rejected more than a thousand times. And how Walt Disney was told he had no creative ideas. These stories gave me a lot of confidence! I mean, chomping on KFC and rolling around Disneyland are a kid's dream! And so I learned this lesson, fast: what other people do or say to you is of literally *no* consequence. It can't touch you! Rejections are just words spoken by people who do not know any better than you. And thank God Sanders and Walt didn't give up, eh?

Rejection is an illusion. Can you feel this way about rejection when it happens to you, too? Can you make your goal more important than your sensitivity, even when the rejection makes you want to scream? The world might not see you in the way you want to be seen yet, but stay in the game, and more will unfold for you eventually. But nobody will ever see you for who you are if you stop too soon!

Now, as a full-time entrepreneur who's in the media quite a lot, I'm rejected *all the time* (*So what?*)! I still receive a lot of silence in response to my pitches and get lots of notes from editors writing back, "I'm passing on this."

That's okay! Great! Pass it is. I'm not giving up. Sometimes, when I get a rejection email, I even laugh a little to myself. Weird, right? I think, *How funny... this person thinks I'm gonna stop here! Ha!*

I really wanted to be a guest writer for a huge business site a few years back. I emailed the editor six times. No response. Most people would have given up. But the editor responded on my seventh try. Now I write for them a lot, and the editor is one of my closest friends. When she wasn't responding, I could've thought things like: *She thinks I'm stupid,* or *She thinks my writing sample isn't good enough or my ideas suck.* Instead I just kept emailing her.

The truth is, when we're blown off, the vast majority of the time *it is not even about us.* The person who rejects us is simply focused on other things. What we perceive as rejection is often not rejection at all, just not the right timing. If I made it all about me and my bad ideas, I would be crazily self-indulgent. Think about what a person has going on in their life — a sick kid, trying to pay the Visa bill, a cranky spouse, a party to plan for an unappreciative relative, fear of losing their job, self-loathing after eating too much lasagna, and the list goes on forever. So it's absurd to think that someone who doesn't even know you is obsessed with rejecting you.

It's nonsense! Yes, you're important. But no one is sitting there conjuring up fantastic ways to reject you. So chill out.

When you realize this, it's like having a protective positivity bubble encase you. People won't get it — and some might think you're naive. Let them! *This is your life.* If you can lessen your fear of rejection even a little, amazing things will start to happen. I guarantee it. Why? Because you'll come to understand more and more that rejection is just a temporary feeling.

And what drives our feelings? Our thoughts. The good news? A thought can change. The most confident among us know this. We just don't fear negative feelings as much. That's the secret. We're willing to feel them and be uncomfortable. We're willing to be visible. We're willing to have people reject us.

Having and Being Enough

When we're able to allow, even welcome, scary feelings, a whole world of possibilities belongs to us. We're unstoppable and untouchable.

And as a result, we do more. We ask for more. We get out there more. We go for more. And we kick ass. It's not the most special, talented, charming, or intelligent among us who win (hey, look at all those folks with PhDs out there who aren't satisfied!) — it's those of us who are *willing to feel the stuff* we all fear. Not being good enough. Not having enough. Not being loved. In his book *What Happy People Know*, Dan Baker breaks this down brilliantly.

He says that unless your fear is a protective force that stops you from doing something dangerous (like swimming in dark water where sharks have been reported), then all fears belong in two buckets. Yes, just *two buckets!* Our fears can be attributed to one of the following:

1. I am not enough.
2. I do not have enough.

As human beings, we haven't really evolved. Back in the days of the cavepeople, these fears were very real. The result of them being actualized was certain death. If you weren't fit, healthy, and strong, the tribe would leave you behind in order to survive. And if you didn't have enough — meaning if you did not collect food every day (or if you collected the wrong berries) or were unable to find the materials to give you shelter and warmth — you would perish.

And today?

Feeling like you're enough in today's world doesn't mean just having the ability to survive, it means being educated, connected, charming, smart, good-looking, thin, interesting…the list is endless, especially when you're busy comparing yourself to your peers.

Having enough means possessing not only the basics like food and shelter but also luxury items. Some of these we can enjoy, but they can also really trap us. For many, having enough means owning a large home, a fancy car, a great closet, vacations to Positano and the French Riviera, keeping up with our friends, and *dropping cash we don't have on stuff we don't need.*

Our circumstances are very different now, but those two innate reptilian brain fears, "I am not enough" and "I do not have enough," remain the same.

Try it out for a second.

Observe any fear in your life, strong or subtle, and you'll be able to attribute it to one of these two fear groups.

> "I can't tell that person I like them; they couldn't possibly be attracted to me!"
>
> "I can't ask for more money at work; it's not like I'm perfect at my job."
>
> "Who am I to start a business?"
>
> "I can't start a blog — no one wants to hear what I have to say."

"I don't want to go to that party. I'm not good with
   new people."

Sound familiar? These are all examples of "I am not enough."
And what about these?

"Money is hard to come by."
"Seth comes from a better family than I do. I'm kinda
   embarrassed to introduce him to my parents."
"Better to stick to the career I know than take a risk
   doing what I'd really love to do, go broke, and be a
   laughingstock."
"Greg makes a lot more money than I do and always
   has nice things. I just feel like he's better than me."
"I won't buy that item that I've been needing for a while
   — I don't want to part with my hard-earned money.

They are all examples of "I do not have enough."

Not all these examples will come down to fear for everyone. Perhaps you don't want to go to the party simply because
you're an introvert and love staying home. Maybe you would
rather postpone a purchase so that you can save for an upcom-
ing vacation. But only *you* know the true motivation behind
the statements you make or the thoughts you think. If your
soul is stirred with a reason for not doing something that feels
right and fair, great. If not, if your decisions leave you feeling insecure, small, and unsatisfied, fear has got you wrapped
around its little finger, my friend.

In understanding this, maybe we don't have to fear being
afraid so much. When a scary feeling pops up, you can soothingly say to yourself, "It's okay. Being scared is normal. Which
of the two buckets can I put this feeling in? I have a good handle on this, though. I'm okay."

Reframing Rejection

This "rejection reframing" is such a brilliant success tool that if it were taught in schools, more of the hidden treasure within us would see the light of day. Because we'd be self-directed. Self-approved. Not plodding along at a snail's pace, hoping not to stand out or upset anyone. Being rejection-proof would be the most important gift I'd give a child if I ever had one. Creativity, smarts, enthusiasm…they all get dampened and reduced by the fear of rejection.

Once you learn how to reframe any rejection that comes your way, you'll find it works with almost all feelings of loss, like:

You didn't get the job…

Belief: I was rejected. I knew I wasn't qualified enough. Perhaps I should look for jobs that pay less and are easier to get.

Truth: Maybe you can polish your interview skills a bit? It's good feedback. Or you can think, *That was a lucky escape! Hey, the boss seemed like a control freak anyway, right?*

You lost your coat…

Belief: I am an idiot.

Truth: But that coat had a hole in it, right? And you needed a new one.

Or your umbrella?

Belief: Yep, there's a part of my brain missing. Why am I always losing umbrellas? Do I drink too much? Is the drinking killing my brain cells and that's why I can't remember my umbrella? Or where I put my keys?

Truth: It's just an umbrella! Maybe someone else needed it! Hey, it wouldn't cry over you.

DIRECT MESSAGE

I freaked out once when I thought I had lost my beloved pair of Krewe sunglasses. Woe was me all morning. I called the barre studio to see if I left them there. I checked every handbag and pocket. I thought they were gone forever! It's okay to take a moment to be upset about losing something you really loved, even if it's just an object. I came to terms with it, thanking them for making me feel fab while they lasted and for adding some snazz to my snaps with my friends. But then I moved the *eff on*, with a sigh. Minutes after accepting my life without my beloved sunglasses, I found them in my junk drawer. Despair does nothing. But acceptance can make you lucky!

Your friend didn't text back about making plans...

Belief: Sara's mad at me.

Truth: Chill! You're still just as close as you were two days ago! Sara's busy on a work deadline today. Maybe she has PMS, or her newborn is keeping her up at night, and her husband hasn't been pulling his weight. Don't make assumptions!

You were ghosted...

Belief: I'll never find love. I'm not attractive enough.

Truth: Now you don't have to waste any more time on that flip-flopper. Time to swipe right on someone else!

Reframing can help you keep your life on track, no matter what shitty thing happens, minor or otherwise. When a friend of mine lost her phone at a bar, she was phoneless for two whole days. She said it was…heaven! She wants to institute a no-phone policy for one day a week because of the freedom it gives her.

"And your screen was broken!" I reminded her. Those grapes *were* sour.

It's up to us to reframe any perceived loss as a positive. Most recently, I severed a friendship and instead of mulling it over and feeling sad, I realized how much lighter and happier I am without this friend in my life (I used to dread our lunches, during which she complained 65 percent of the time.)

The best news? Nature abhors a vacuum. It's a universal law. That means that empty spaces fill quickly, but only when we let go. The person with the reframe controls their world. Nothing much can affect them. External bad things that happen impact them less. They're not as much at the mercy of mistakes or disappointments. They're too busy approving of reality. And when you accept and approve of what's happening, even if you don't like it to begin with, you're rockin' some real self-approval (and sanity).

Consider this. When you feel rejected, you're actually living in the past. Yep.

That remark someone made about your killer outfit that hurt you? *That was last weekend, dude.*

The email saying, "No, thank you very much" to your awesome offer — check your email. That was yesterday.

That brunch you're viewing on Instagram where you were left off the group text chain? That was weeks ago.

Remember teary Tina who was upset that Jenna called her a copycat? Yep, she learned that some old gossip was meaningless, and you can, too. In fact, right now, in this moment, nothing and no one is rejecting you. *You're rejecting yourself over and over by reliving it.* Stop! Look out the window at the sky. Go for a short, brisk walk. Watch a funny YouTube video. Call an upbeat friend. Give yourself some perspective in knowing that you and your rejection aren't even a speck in the universe or human history! Get over it!

You're doing great at life. Foster this perspective. You won't care about or remember this in the future. So why keep it alive now? Don't let one thing going wrong in your day color the eight things that are going right.

And consider this for a second. How many times have you looked back and realized the job, the love interest, the apartment were not meant to be yours because something much better arrived afterward? I can say "check!" to hundreds of these experiences. It makes me laugh (often with relief) now. Rejection helps us evaluate. I was fired from my first full-time job as a receptionist at a car dealership in Chatswood, Sydney. It went a little like this:

"Susie, Greg [the general manager] would like to see you." My heart seized in my chest. "This is *it!*" I thought to myself. I'm getting promoted!

I was young, naive, ambitious — and yes, a little (a lot) cocky — when I started out in my career. I joined in an entry-level receptionist role, and I was desperate to get into sales. (Hey, *The Magic of Thinking Big* had left an indelible mark on me — what can I say?) I spent all my time with the sales team, listening to them, helping them with their clients, upselling on things like plush floor mats or leather seating whenever I had the chance. It felt so fun to me. Whenever someone would come into the dealership who wasn't being attended to, I'd start pitching the different makes and models of the cars to them instead of doing my *actual* job, which was answering the phone and doing data entry.

"They *have* to be noticing this great work!" I kept saying rather confidently to myself (while totally ignoring what I was supposed to be doing). One time, when the phone rang, I even said to a colleague, "Can you get that?" Like I said...young and cocky!

So when the big boss wanted to see me, I was ready.

I threw on a dab of lip gloss and strutted up those stairs, prepared to gracefully accept my promotion to salesperson. Oh, and I was going to request business cards, too (in my mind, business cards meant that you had hit the *big* time). I was thinking, *Should I put my married or maiden name on my cards? Remember to negotiate their offer, don't be too quick to accept. Let them work for it.*

As soon as my butt hit the chair these words slapped me in the face: "Susie, there's no easy way to say this. We're letting you go. It's not working out."

Full-body sting. Breathing stopped. Heart sank. Whaaat?!?!

I hate repetitive tasks, I am not detail oriented, and I was lousy in a support role. The rejection made me realize what I am not suited to and made me assess what I am good at, fast. That day, I was surprised to be kicked out, but I wasn't sad (although I did feel sad that I'd just bought a case of Diet Coke and put it under my desk and knew I wouldn't get it back. I did entertain the idea of going back to pick it up, but my mom texted, "Don't you dare — have some class!").

The even bigger silver lining was that the temp agency that placed me there ended up hiring me as a recruiter, because the owner saw my sales potential after I told her the truth about what happened. I never looked back. Rejection doesn't place a scarlet letter on your chest! And ever since then, my jobs have been overall pretty great. I needed the wake-up call to get me out of what was a completely unsuitable role. Rejection can make you act! Because the universe will often do for you what you won't do for yourself. And this sometimes shows up as a big, fat dismissal. So congratulations!

We're not here on the planet just to observe and feel. We are here to *create and do*! And you'll never get busy creating the present while holding on to the energy of past hurts. So slip straight into that positivity, blinders-on bubble. Shed the nonsense that's already over. Stuff not going your way doesn't have to hurt you for long. And other people don't have to scare you. They're just like you with only two real fears, remember?

Sing it, Elsa. Let it go!

Check this:

❑ Recall your own sour-grapes story by writing down three times you were rejected in the past. What were the ultimate outcomes? What were the hidden blessings? What good came out of something you perceived as bad?

❑ The next time a fear thought plagues you, observe it. Put it into one of the two buckets: "I am not enough" and "I do not have enough." Notice how simple your fears are at their base level.

❑ Understand that rejection is not personal. And that you do not have to set yourself up to suffer for nothing. It's just the opinion of one person. You can appeal it. There will be many other responses out there. Exhale!

CHAPTER TWELVE

Ask

If you don't ask, the answer is always no.

ANONYMOUS

One night when I was in my early twenties, my friend and I were debating whether to go to a Sneaky Sound System concert at the Hordern Pavilion in Sydney. We almost didn't go, but at the last minute we decided to stop by. I spotted a tall, handsome guy in the crowd and was pleased when we started chatting. He made me laugh, and he seemed very genuine and warm. Many women I know would have waited for him to make some kind of move. But he didn't, so before I left, I asked him, "How about you take my number?"

He did — and called the next day. We have been married for more than a decade.

How did I end up in one of the happiest, most compatible

marriages I know? Because in 2007, I asked a single question of a handsome stranger at a concert.

Where might asking a single question lead *you?*

Don't underestimate the power of a well-timed question. Big or small, questions create opportunities. They open up dialogue between people. They make invisible doors open. And they have another important function, too: they stop you from making assumptions.

Too easily, we assume that someone would not be interested in us. That the nice table near the window at a restaurant is reserved for someone else. That someone is upset with us if they don't text us back the same day. Assumptions are dangerous because when we make them, we often create suffering before we even know anything for sure.

My friend Bianca told me once that she was sitting by the pool at a beautiful resort in Hawaii and wasn't super happy with her cabana but didn't feel confident enough to ask the staff if she could change. *Are you serious?* I thought to myself. This woman is a multimillionaire, powerhouse businesswoman, and she was too afraid to ask if she could move seats.

In his book *The Four Agreements*, Don Miguel Ruiz says, "Don't make assumptions. Find the courage to ask questions and to express what you really want. Communicate with others as clearly as you can to avoid misunderstandings, sadness, and drama. With just this one agreement, you can completely transform your life."

Negotiate for More

In my job as a recruitment consultant (for that temp agency that saw my potential), I saw a load of salary negotiations. I learned the value of a good employee, quickly. I remember one particular time when a candidate was offered two executive assistant positions, and so she had her pick of both. This woman was calm, professional, and polite — but she also really knew her worth. She asked us to negotiate not only more money but a host of other benefits, too, like leaving early on Thursdays to attend something at her kid's school, and budget approval for some training to keep her PowerPoint and Excel skills sharp.

She got it all.

And let me tell you something else: she was up against more experienced candidates. But her self-approving, confident style made her appear even more valuable to the hiring managers. Because if we dig ourselves, we set the tone for other people to dig us, too. It's like, "This one's putting in requests. She must have the goods!"

Since then, I've negotiated my salary up front every time when accepting a new job *and* each time I have had increased responsibility and/or success. I knew how loyal and hardworking an employee I was, so I always asked for what I felt was fair. Negotiating became a fun game, and one I'd almost always win. As a result, I've earned the same as (if not more than) some of my male counterparts. *Just because I asked.* Yes, the scary ten-minute conversation can put you off, but think of the long term! It's beyond worth it.

DIRECT MESSAGE

Next time a scary conversation you want to have makes you want to turn and run, think of this quote from author Tim Ferriss in his book *The 4-Hour Workweek*: "A person's success in life can usually be measured by the number of uncomfortable conversations he or she is willing to have."

Know this: No one's gonna throw money at you if they think you're happy where you're at. You have to bring your worth to their attention. As author Elizabeth Gilbert says, "Success isn't passive. You must participate relentlessly in the manifestation of your own blessings."

When people have come to me for coaching in asking for a salary increase, they often assume the percentage increase the company is willing to give is pretty low. I question it and dare them to aim higher (in a negotiation, that leaves some nice wiggle room). It's an easy assumption to make when we're scared to be asking in the first place. So if you bring your A game to the office every day, you know that you provide a lot of value with the work you do, and you want to see your efforts reflected in your bank account, you're probably in a great position to ask for more.

There's major evidence that those of us who don't constantly negotiate our salaries leave millions of dollars on the table over the course of our career. In *Women Don't Ask*, Linda Babcock and Sara Laschever reveal that "a woman who routinely negotiates her salary increases will earn over one million dollars more by the time she retires than a woman who accepts what she's offered every time without asking for more."

Let that sink in for a second. And then remember, *that's just the money*. When you don't ask, you're missing out on loads of benefits, such as opening up career-acceleration dialogue and illustrating your achievements to management. However unfairly, in a lot of cases, the most visible among us get the promotions in the workplace. When you're asking, you're visible. And you're touting yourself. You need no one else's approval to do this. It's you that has to speak up for and represent you.

Young children know this, right? They don't stop asking. I was always asking my mom for something — more time outside, an ice cream from the ice-cream man ("too expensive!"), to have a sick day from school. Sometimes I was lucky, sometimes not. My mom could be a no-nonsense woman. But I do remember lining up for a cone barefoot and being elated at least once at getting a fake sick day.

By the way, I've included a proven, successful script for asking for a raise at the end of this book that you can use and reuse whenever you need it! It's time tested and industry tested, and it does not change.

Feeling scared about doing something, like asking for more money?

Remember that photo of yourself as a kid we looked at earlier? Do it for her. She's relying on you. Becoming someone who asks for things isn't about changing your personality. It's about changing your acceptance of, and comfort with, the real you. The real you who knows that she deserves good things.

Remember: if you don't ask, the answer is always no.

What are you not asking for right now? What comes to mind?

Let's throw in some much-needed perspective here. The reason you don't want to ask? Don't hide behind "I'm happy with everything I have," okay?

It's a nerve-racking thing to voice a question, I know. I still feel it myself all the time. I know what it's like to feel left hanging for even a second and risk being shut down. I test myself all the time with things that are 100 percent going to be a no just to remind myself that it's just a temporary, uneasy feeling that waves through me. It doesn't control my life! And it can't hurt me. And it doesn't even last for long.

When I was a teenager, I worked at a department store selling perfume. Each "house" (Estée Lauder, Clinique, YSL) had a promotional window every few months, which meant if you spent a certain amount with that brand, you got a gift.

Whoever had the promotional window going on always had the most sales that week. It was exciting! But there was one house that was never on promotion: Chanel.

"Chanel is never, ever, on promotion," my dolled-up, serious manager told me when I started.

Oooh, I thought. Chanel must be the best. It doesn't discount itself or throw in free goodies because it knows it's enough. I wanted to be like Chanel when I was an adult.

And just for fun — and never-ending self-stretching — whenever I purchase something now from the iconic brand, either in a Chanel store or shopping at the glass counters I used to stand on the other side of, I ask, "Is there anything you can do for me, something else we can throw in?" I'm met with either a tiny fragrance sample or more frequently a smile and a simple "sorry."

I know Chanel will say no, and that's why I do it. Because it's okay with me to be turned down. It's a great ongoing confidence test. The mini knock-backs don't hurt me. As far as I can tell, I'm still alive and well. Because no is just nothing. Think about that word. It's *no thing*. Just a concept you can accept or reject. *Next!*

DIRECT MESSAGE

Remember that fear of failure is more about how others perceive us than it is about the failure itself, so props if you try a Chanel-counter type of antic in front of a friend! I do it in front of Heath. He's so used to me, he doesn't even roll his eyes anymore.

Everyone Is Worthy of Asking and Receiving

I have an important question for you: Do you feel guilty about receiving? Be honest, now. There's great irony here because we're probably so willing to give, right? A client once said to me, "I'm really happy to help anyone out, but I couldn't possibly ask for help back." *Why not?*

If you don't feel worthy of receiving, you need to learn to love yourself. *Everyone is worthy of asking and receiving.* Even in the smallest cases, like when someone offers to put your heavy-ass carry-on in the overhead bin on a plane. Or when someone waits and holds the elevator open for you as you collect your mail. We're not supposed to go through life without the help of one another. We're supposed to support each other. And that takes place through dynamic exchange.

In nature, all things support all things. In Deepak Chopra's *The Seven Spiritual Laws of Success*, law number two is the law of giving. Here's what he says about it as it pertains to receiving: "Every relationship is one of give and take. Giving engenders receiving, and receiving engenders giving. What goes up must come down; what goes out must come back. In reality, receiving is the same thing as giving, because giving and receiving are different aspects of the flow of energy in the universe. And if you stop the flow of either, you interfere with nature's intelligence."

I don't know about you, but I'm not monkeying with nature's intelligence. I want to delight in giving *and* receiving to keep the flow fresh and easy. So I frequently ask someone taller if they can help get my carry-on into the overhead bin. And I'll holler, "Can you hold the door?" to a neighbor when I'm scooping up my mail. I'll also do the same for them. Remember: they can say no if they want, and so can you. Is it rejection if a neighbor is busy and doesn't feel like holding the elevator door? Heck, no! You can dismiss it as easily as I dismiss an editor not responding to my emails. It's all okay.

"How Can I Let This Be Easier?"

I have a personal mantra that I use again and again: *How can I let this be easier?* This perspective is so simple but can feel really revolutionary. Yes, we can drink the wheatgrass, do the yoga, rock the meditation apps…but what about thinking to ourselves, *How can I let my life be easier?*

This mantra can be used anywhere. When you're having a conversation with your partner. Dealing with those pesky flight delays. Experiencing a regular day at work. Driving somewhere new. Pitching your stories to the media. Making dinner. Taking on a big scary project or writing a book.

It's a gorgeous, life-altering question if ever there was one. And it's one of my fave life-coaching questions to ask any human being having any struggle! *We do not have to make everything so hard.* Please read that again.

Let me give you some examples of things I've asked for:

1. My husband to take my number (the best request of my life)! I'm grateful for this every day.
2. Relatives to lovingly adjust their expectations around communication. When we moved to New York, I had an honest, wonderful conversation with my awesome mother-in-law explaining that with the big time difference and our new schedules, it's not always easy to Skype every weekend. I didn't want her to be sad or feel neglected. It went so well, and we all felt relieved!
3. The table I want in a restaurant. Everyone pays the same, so I like to request a window table or cozy corner spot.

4. Coffee with someone I want to meet.

5. A little more kindness from a woman I saw being rude to a yoga studio assistant.

6. More reliability from a guy I used to date (he never could give that, and the relationship was short-lived — better to know sooner, my loves).

7. What I need from my husband on a regular basis (I love quality downtime together, and I'm specific about how it looks).

8. My well-meaning mom friends (or anyone, for that matter) to stop asking when I'm going to have a baby. Or to stop saying that I'll regret it if I don't!

9. Directions — constantly. And a request to not use words like *west* or *yards*. Please just point and say how many minutes it'll take! (By the way, I'll never get over how many men would rather drive for forty-five minutes in circles than ask for directions from another driver!)

10. Clarity on expectations from managers (ambiguity in the workplace is rampant).

11. Free late checkouts at a hotel — 90 percent of the time this works. I also always ask for the nicest room possible in the tier that we've booked.

12. Punctuality (since when is it okay to be so damn late?)!

13. If I may go first in a group presentation setting — to get it out of the way and calm my nerves.

14. Clarity from myself. I'll ask, "What the *hell* am I doing? This *needs* to change!" This question comes up when my life needs a course correct. Wrong relationship, wrong job, too much partying. You have to get real with yourself every so often.

15. Forgiveness — many times. This has been perhaps

the most important request of my life. Getting angry too fast over something small like losing my computer charger. Drinking too much some days. Letting a silly fight with my sister go on for *years*. I eff up a lot. The older I get, the sooner I own it.

I'd love to illustrate here the power of appreciation and forgiveness between my parents.

My dad's last words to me were, "Appreciate yourself, my loving clone." He wrote it to me in a letter for my nineteenth birthday. As a high school teacher and author, he was very proud of me when he saw I loved to write. I looked like him *and* shared his passion for words. Now when I think of him, I think of the five-year-old boy who was sent to boarding school and escaped to walk home to his mum, as he put it. He had no idea of the distance. The police found him and took him back to school, and he cried, "I just want to see my mum for a minute!" I'm happy they're together now.

I appreciated my dad's courage in *just going for it* when we'd go swimming at the beach. He'd swim so far out that we couldn't see him anymore. My sister and I would shout, "Come back, Dad! There are sharks!" We thought he was so strong, and he was. He'd say, "Punch me as hard as you can in the stomach!" My sister wouldn't. I would. He wouldn't flinch. He'd also pick us up with his baby finger.

I felt pride during his sober stints, when he'd come to my primary school to teach us how to play chess. And then later, looking at old photos of him as a boxer before his addiction began.

My mom was the last person to see him before he died. Even though they could never make their relationship work, she traveled by train to see him when he had just days to live.

When she got the call, she didn't even brush her hair before leaving the house. She threw her wallet into her handbag and walked to the train station. It meant so much to her, and I'm sure it did to him, in the end. He said he wasn't scared to die because he had me and my sister. To me, it's an illustration of the core truth in this world. That only love is real in the end. And that our only job is forgiveness. After court battles, abuse, affairs, and mistresses, unspeakable insults — in the end, my mom and dad were loving to each other.

I challenge you to ask for five things this week. Forgiveness might be one of the big things you've been waiting for. But even asking for something as small as a window seat in a restaurant counts!

Once you start asking, you start getting. And everyone wonders what's changed. It's your level of self-approval and the acknowledgment of your worthiness being on the rise. And yes, it can be that easy. When you attempt it just five times, you'll see.

DIRECT MESSAGE

Here's a pro tip: using the word *because* helps you be really persuasive when asking for anything at all. No matter what follows it, your request appears more justified and thought through. And to be extra polite, opening a request with "Would it be possible for..." makes a big difference. For example: "Would it be possible for me to take the corner table, please? Because this lunch is a special occasion."

There's no such thing as a bad outcome. Did you get shut down? *Congrats*. You still did it. It's not about the result. It's about you stepping into the truth that you're bigger than whatever scares you.

Bottom line, don't be afraid to ask. And if someone offers you help before you ask for it — take it! And appreciate it. It's special. Accepting help honors the giver. It's a gift, so accept it with grace. My mom told me a story about her neighbor in Poland who came into a crisis when his horse unexpectedly died. Roman was a kind neighbor and needed the horse to work on his small farm. Roman knew that my mom's father came into a small sum of money after selling a calf that same week. Before Roman asked my grandfather for a dime (well, a Polish zloty!), my grandfather told him, "I know what happened to your horse. I'll lend you some money." Can you imagine how happy Roman felt? Don't deny yourself the pleasure in this world of not just receiving but giving, too.

Check this:

❏ What are you not asking for right now? Journal for a few minutes on what comes to mind.

❏ If asking feels uncomfortable to you (and you feel awkward or guilty about receiving), consider: *How can I let this be easier?*

❏ Ask for five things this week, regardless of perceived outcome.

❏ Give something unexpected to someone who needs it this week.

❏ If it's relevant to you, read the script at the back of this book on how to ask for a raise.

CHAPTER THIRTEEN

Let It Be Easy

*Always believe that something wonderful
is about to happen.*

SUKHRAJ DHILLON

When I was a kid, I dreamed of living in "the place with the big buildings." I didn't even know it was called New York back then. And as I've mentioned earlier, when I was twenty-five and Heath was twenty-three, out of the blue he was offered a job in New York City. We had to move in two weeks… and we did it and never looked back. That was more than ten years ago.

I used to think it could never happen. America is an impossible place to get a visa (especially for me, without a college degree). But it happened. And a few years after that we — equally surprisingly! — were given green cards.

Can we revisit that mantra from the last chapter for a second and ask, *How can we let our day-to-day existence be easier?*

Because the truth is, it's never about the situation you're facing. It's what you're *believing* about the situation that will make it difficult. Wayne Dyer said, "There is no stress in this world. Only stressful thoughts." Wait. Could you be making *many* pretty easy situations stressful…just with your thoughts? Could that be true? Let that sink in for a second. It's a dramatic shift, right? What if there were no stress? It may seem impossible (and in some cases it might be), but what if making this shift in your thinking could actually reduce your stress? You'd be a magnet for new, exciting opportunities! The easiest way to do this is to change your mindset by watching your words.

Brain coach Jim Kwik taught me a good lesson: he said to replace your "to-do" list with a *"get-to-do"* list. Even for just the next twenty-four hours, can you watch your words and how you speak about what you "get" to do? Are you grateful for the job that means you need an early alarm, grateful for the spouse who burnt the chicken, grateful for the legs that let you dance to Taylor Swift (even though you're tired and don't want to go to dance class)? Notice how appreciation can nudge you into ease mode!

To build on this mantra, there's a question I ask myself whenever I'm taking on a new project or handling an annoying daily situation like being one ingredient short for dinner. It's a gorgeous question that can simplify whatever feels overwhelming: *What's essential here?*

"What's Essential Here?"

Here are some examples of how I use this question:

Task: You are preparing to give a presentation in front of a group. Depending on your comfort level when it comes to public speaking, your stress level could be as high as a 10!

Questions to ask yourself:

- **How can I make this easier (or simpler)?** Can you reuse old slides? Keep the presentation itself as short as it can be, and leave time for Q&A (which requires no additional preparation from you)?
- **What's essential here?** Only include the essential information! No bells and whistles. Good enough is good enough.

> **DIRECT MESSAGE**
>
> Whenever I'm asked to speak or present something, when possible I like to turn it into a Q&A instead. There's no prep work for me, and it's more interactive that way. It's so easy, it feels like cheating — but it's not!

Task: You need a little detox because you've been overeating and drinking (but still have a busy social calendar).

Questions to ask yourself:

- **How can I make this easier (or simpler)?** Can you cancel some of the less important events in your calendar? Instead of freaking out, overspending on health-cleansing products or supplements, and being a hermit for a week, can you eat a tad more cleanly throughout the day, have a two-glass-of-wine maximum at night, and set yourself a decent time to be home? Hey — participate in your life! It's all temporary.
- **What's essential here?** Rest and water? Great! Be sure to be in bed by 10:00 PM and always have a bottle of eau

at the ready. Maybe you have three or four big things going on this week. What are the most essential two? Don't feel bad about rescheduling stuff. Almost everyone is secretly relieved when that happens.

Task: You have to have a serious talk with a relative or your spouse that feels uncomfortable.

Questions to ask yourself:

- **How can I make this easier (or simpler)?** Remember, you two love each other, right? Communication is a core part of expressing that love. Can you make it feel less foreboding in your mind and more like, "I'm happy to be working this out! It'll be good for us." And can you do it over cake? And with a smile?

- **What's essential here?** You have something to say, right? Great! Keep it simple. Share your point of view, then listen (really listen). I bet that you two agree on far more than you disagree on. Say, for example, you don't like your spouse's overspending. I'm sure you both want a healthy savings account, enough money for holidays, and shrinking debt on those credit cards, right? Great! Start there. What's essential in achieving that together? Maybe less shopping…but she can still occasionally add to her sneaker collection.

The message here: lighten up.

Why? When we're heavy, serious, or stressed-out, we're closed off not just from recognizing the good in our lives but from allowing more good in, too. From getting that next break. Remember those mirror neurons? It's like constantly wearing this big, inflatable sumo suit that repels opportunities. Hold on to this image in your mind for a minute because we're going to be using it again soon.

When you see everything through a filter of pressure or burden, are you allowing yourself to be happy in this moment? No? Well, that's a disaster because *this moment* is your life! And stress is blinding you.

What are you so afraid of, exactly? Question it! You can keep asking, "And then what will happen?" when questioning the downward spiral of thoughts that just make you feel worse and worse as the seconds pass by. I used to worry about losing every job I ever had (I think this is a pretty universal concern). It made me feel hopeless, not to mention anxious, when I'd think about it. My thoughts would run like this:

If I were to be fired today, would I still be alive? Yes. And if so, would I be living under a bridge? Probably not. This is where perspective matters above all. Losing a job is often much more bearable than the months — even years — of fear that precede it.

Shawn Achor says, "Adversities, no matter what they are, simply don't hit us as hard as we think they will. Our fear of consequences is always worse than the consequences themselves." Because things are rarely as bad as we make them out to be in our minds.

DIRECT MESSAGE

What consequences are you fearing right now? The fear is the real problem here, not the possibility of them happening. Because you'll handle it. Read that again. You've handled everything hard in your life so far, right? You've survived! Why would that change now?

Opening to Possibility

The best ideas and moments of inspiration come to us when we have a calm, optimistic mindset. Stress crushes this. Ironically, our ideas, judgments, and ability to think are why we are employed in the first place! Who needs a scary boss when you're doing a perfect job of freaking yourself out all on your own?

And here's the sad news: stress in the present moment means that we often write ourselves and our dreams off before we even begin. We're never open to possibilities that surround us because of that heavy, repelling sumo suit. One time a friend of mine — an editor of an overseas in-flight airline magazine — told me a simple story, which illustrates this idea perfectly.

A fancy watch brand was running a contest. Thousands of people saw the contest, but only thirteen people ended up entering it. It was a simple, short question-and-answer survey that would take three to four minutes to complete. So there ended up being a 1 in 13 chance of winning a $10,000 watch! Pretty good odds, if you ask me.

Since hearing that story, I've thought, what haven't I put my hat in the ring for? What have I been blind to that could've been easy? Probably a whole lot. It's a tragic thing to go through life with blinders on because you're just trying to make it through the (tough) week. I don't want a fancy watch, but there's plenty of other stuff I want, as well as plenty of other opportunities. We just need to open our eyes and look because a lot of what we want and need is probably more available than we might assume.

Starting my coaching business meant that I identified a big opportunity that helped me scale, fast. I sometimes used to waste whole afternoons bored in my cubicle, reading cool websites like MindBodyGreen. I could spend hours clicking on articles with titles like "Five Ways to Sleep Better" or "Eight Tips for Meditating When Your Mind Is Racing." One day I started paying more attention: *Who is writing these?* I'd think. *Because I have some useful stuff to say, too!*

I'd notice that some of the writers were coaches. And I was a life coach in training! Because of this — with no formal qualifications, writing experience, or connections (and without overthinking it, which is the real key) — I submitted five hundred words.

Two weeks later, I was published. *I had an author page!* I knew from my dad, who was a local history author, that the word *author* is derived from the word *authority*. I felt *so* legit and proud and fancy and established and famous. The article was shared nearly four thousand times. And I didn't even have a website! When it comes to the order of how you "should" do things, why not just go for it anyway and say: *So what?*

As a result of remaining more open to all the opportunities that exist in the world, I've gotten some of the coolest media coverage in the world — like being on the *Today* show; and writing for Oprah.com, *Business Insider*, *Forbes*, and *Entrepreneur*; and even becoming the resident life coach at one of the world's biggest health and wellness sites for millennials, Greatist, where millions of people read my weekly column, all of which catapulted my business.

And here's the thing, I never completed my life coaching certification!

This break for me wouldn't have happened if I had been thinking, *There are twenty-five gazillion life coaches out there. I'm not certified. I'll never get clients.* Because when you're stressed and in self-doubt, you deflect opportunity. What if, like the fancy watch contest and my media submission, the odds for what you want are actually better than you think? Don't leave those longings unattended, my friend! Your desires matter.

Can you suspend your disbelief and think for a second, *What might I be a single break away from?* What might a phone call, an email, or a chance encounter do for you? What if it's on its way? Believing is essential. And think: What good has come into your life with ease so far — perhaps a pregnancy, a great apartment, a best friend, a cool career offer? Not everything good that's come to you was a struggle, right? So why would it have to be now?

"What's the Advantage of...?"

Look, I know you might be scared. Being open to new things takes courage. You have to remind yourself that you're worth it. And that, most of the time, it's safe "out there." If you feel blocked and unable to receive, ask yourself this question:

What's the (secret) benefit of staying where I am?

On the surface, there might not be one. But if you go a little deeper, there's probably something that scares you. Earlier in my business, I worked through this question with my tapping coach Greg (if you haven't tried EFT, Emotional Freedom Technique, yet, it's amazing — start with a free YouTube video from my friend Brad Yates). I felt like I couldn't make a business decision, and my indecision was keeping me stuck, frustrated, and irritated with myself.

He asked about the options I had before me, my feelings about each potential outcome, and then...he asked the magical question that changed everything:

"What is the advantage of staying blocked, Susie?"

Whaaat, Greg? I thought. *Advantage of being blocked? There is none! Zip! Zero. Is he crazy? Man, I need a new coach.*

Until…I thought about it. Really thought. After some contemplation, I knew the answer. *Being blocked was a wonderful excuse for not taking any action.* Meaning that if I didn't make a decision and act, I could not fail. My "block" was a defensive emotion to keep me safe. Even though inaction is never safe, really (my logical mind knows it's a form of action, too, and often the worst kind), my subconscious knew the decision was a big one for me, so it put a block into my thinking.

> **DIRECT MESSAGE**
>
> Being blocked is a wonderful excuse for not taking any action.

"I guess the upside would be that if I don't make a choice, I can't screw things up, at least in the short term," I said.

Now, as a coach myself, I have used this question repeatedly with my clients (and myself!). Here are some of the ways it's popped up in my conversations:

What's the advantage of *not* getting healthy?

Reactive answer: There isn't one! I do want to get healthy, it's just hard!

Deeper answer: If I'm overweight and single, it means that's the reason why I'm single. It means there's nothing more serious wrong with me.

What's the advantage of comparing yourself with your college friends (and feeling competitive with and distant from them)?

Reactive answer: Who can help comparing themselves to their friends? I don't want to feel competitive, but who can help it?

Deeper answer: If I keep them at arm's length, they won't see my flaws. I feel behind and sad, and I don't want them to really see me. I feel that parts of me are totally inadequate.

What's the advantage of *not* asking for a raise?

Reactive answer: I'm not the kind of person who can just ask for a raise. Plus, my company doesn't really have the budget to give raises very often.

Deeper answer: I don't want to be rejected, and if I *do* get the outcome I want, my husband might resent my new income. He's already insecure, and I don't want to rock the boat at home.

What's the advantage of *not* confronting your controlling sister?

Reactive answer: I don't think it will do any good. She won't listen.

Deeper answer: I don't feel like I can stand up for myself. Maybe I'm not good at making my own decisions; perhaps I'd actually be lost without her. I don't actually feel strong or capable enough to run my life on my own.

Do any of these answers sound even remotely familiar?

Uncovering Your Blocks

Where might you be blocked right now? Think about it quietly for three or four minutes. Maybe it's a recent block (an opportunity that's just arisen) or an old block (being stuck in an unhealthy relationship for five years). Ask yourself the following questions, and write down the answers:

- *What's the block?*
- *What's the upside of this block/problem/issue?*
- *What might be keeping me here, if I really think about it and am honest with myself?*
- *What could happen if I lose my belief about this block? How can I see this situation or problem differently?*
- And finally, *If I completely approved of myself, how would this problem change?*

Awareness of our secret beliefs — and the truth behind them — is the first step in reducing their power over us. If they loosened their hold on you, how much closer might that next break of yours be? You can continually bust outta that awful sumo suit by acknowledging how far you've come already.

Digging for Gold

Some time ago, I studied "hedonic adaptation," the tendency of human beings to quickly return to a relatively stable level of happiness, despite major positive or negative events or life changes. For instance, it's amazing how short-lived the happiness rush can be after achieving a big goal, like receiving an awesome gift, getting a series of pay raises, getting engaged, or fitting into an old pair of jeans. There are moments in our lives that fill us with so much joy that we could burst at the seams, right? In those moments, life feels fair, generous, and awesome.

But then what?

Pretty soon, we come back down to earth. The joy seems short-lived, no matter how deeply we longed or how long we waited for the positive thing that finally arrived. Psychologists state that as a result of hedonic adaptation, we revert back to our general baseline of happiness fairly quickly. And this happens when things go wrong, too. There are studies of people who've lost limbs, for example, and after a period of adjustment, they end up just as happy as they used to be.

We get used to good stuff too fast sometimes, when it feels more satisfying to prolong the pleasure. We might love the gift but then start thinking of the next one. The excitement of getting engaged is replaced by wedding-planning anxiety. We love how our jeans fit but then wonder if they could be a size smaller still.

These life changes rapidly become our new normal, and as a result, our aspiration levels continue to rise. Success is a moving target, and therefore, we rarely stay satisfied for long. The truth is that the best parts of our lives are often the most easily overlooked. How can we prevent this? Through serious appreciation of what is. I named this "digging for gold" after an experience with my best friend. Before we went out for the night, she asked to borrow some earrings. "Go ahead," I said. "Go into my jewelry box and take whatever."

She came out of my bedroom wearing some dangly gold earrings I had not worn in probably two years. I forgot I even had them.

"Oh, I love these!" she exclaimed, twisting her head to show them off. "Keep 'em!" I answered. "I don't wear them anyway."

She was delighted.

We went to a party that night, and I was surprised to hear how many compliments those earrings received. *Damn*, I thought. *Maybe I should've kept them.* A couple of days later, I hopped online to get myself another pair, but they had been discontinued. I couldn't get them anymore.

I had to laugh. *It took someone else to show me what I had* — and we're just talking about a dang pair of earrings here. Always looking for the life lesson, I thought, *Where else am I overlooking the gold in my life?*

Open Those Arms Wide

Here's how you can see more of the gold in your life, too. Use this morning ritual, which I based on an old saying I love: "Imagine if you lost everything you had…and then got it back again." I mean, how panicked do you feel sometimes when you've just misplaced your cell phone? Here's the ritual, which I call Open Those Arms Wide.

Take a few deep breaths and imagine if you:

- lost your best friend
- lost a limb
- lost your job
- lost your access to food and water (plenty of people live this way)
- lost your home

List a few other things in your mind that would be devastating to lose. Picture it. Feel it happening. Keep breathing. Notice the emotions of loss that sweep over you when you visualize losing what matters most to you.

Now open your eyes. Look around. It's all still there! Aren't you one lucky soul? Open those arms wide and hug someone or something! You don't need the universe to take something away before you appreciate it, do you?

This exercise is jarring — and gives you a dose of perspective like nothing else.

It's like waking up from a bad dream. Maybe we're in a

strange place and in danger. (I had the worst dream once that I was in *The Hunger Games*.) We're scared, right? We feel all the emotions as if the thing were actually happening. Our body physically responds to the fear.

And then...we wake up!

We're relieved and happy because we're safely in our bed and in no danger at all. Instant happiness, eh? We've awakened from a bad dream. The good news is that awakening comes in many forms. Just as in a dream, a lot of what scares us is not real.

Perspective counts. It shows us what we have, which lights the way for what more could be. It's closer than you think. As Macklemore sings in his song "Glorious," "the world is up for grabs," and he's right. The future belongs to whomever seizes it.

Play the song on Spotify now. "I feel glorious, glorious... Got a chance to start again...I was born for this."

Yes. You were born for endless good things to find you.

Check this:

❏ When faced with a task that overwhelms you, ask yourself: *What's essential here?* It's a great question that can simplify whatever feels overwhelming.

❏ When you're afraid of something bad happening, keep asking, "And then what will happen?" Keep going until you get to the worst-case scenario. Put the truth on paper to get the scaries out of your head.

❏ Set aside a few moments to journal and dream by asking, "What might be just one break away from me?"

❏ Then list (honestly, to yourself) what the secret saboteur could be that's keeping you blocked. Ask yourself:

- *What's my block?*
- *What's the advantage of this block/problem/issue?*
- *What might be keeping me here, if I really think about it and am honest with myself?*
- *What might happen if I lost my belief about this block? How could I see this situation or problem differently?*
- And finally, *If I completely approved of myself and felt worthy of every single thing I want, how would this problem change?*

❏ Do the Open Those Arms Wide ritual three mornings in a row. Notice how your perspective shifts.

CHAPTER FOURTEEN

You're Going to Be Okay

The greatest thing you can give yourself is
freedom from what others think.

ABRAHAM-HICKS

I'll never forget the time that I was walking around the Jackie Onassis Reservoir in Central Park and a woman was walking just in front of me but slightly faster. I sped up to overtake her, and then *she* sped up, then I sped up again, then *she* sped up again. We were both walking comically faster than our normal speed so we wouldn't be in each other's personal space for too long. I finally I gave up and let her go ahead — but then she slowed down. *Did she know we were in a secret race?* Soon she was only a few steps ahead of me again, and I sped up full throttle to overtake her.

Ha! I thought. *I win.*

Until I realized I was so focused on this foolish race that I missed the damn exit path. I had to turn around and walk back, tail between my legs (trying to look as intentional as possible, of course).

Has this been happening to you? Do you focus on other people and then lose your own way? Whether it's something small and silly like an imaginary race or something big like your career and vision for your future, it's easy to follow others and veer off the right path, often with much bigger consequences. And so many of us do that, either accidentally or on purpose.

The only thing wrong with you is the belief that someone else knows better. And the fear of that person's judgment. Or the belief that you must follow or compete with anyone.

Your Unquestionable Worthiness

Is self-approval strutting to the VIP line (even if you're not a "VIP"), asking for a raise, negotiating a discount, raising your hand in an intimidating meeting, asking someone out, wearing a bikini regardless of how your body looks? It can be all those things, yes. But it's also *way* bigger, more important, and more inherent within you than anything tangible, external, or even visible. It's simpler, clearer, and easier to acknowledge in moments of joy...but impossible to let in during moments of doubt. It's something ancient that you feel when you are at your best.

Because it's the most fundamental truth there is: your unquestionable worthiness.

You are worthy, *no matter what*. It's not up for discussion. You didn't ask to be here. But the universal intelligence that created everything also created you. Think of all the incredible things that led up to you being here: your parents meeting, *their* parents meeting — all the components that had to fit together to result in creating you. There are no accidents, and there is nothing you can do that can reduce your worthiness. This permanent, undeletable, fixed worthiness is the only thing that really matters, once you're aware of it. Think — if you found a crisp $100 bill on the street and a crumpled-up one, does their value differ? Not one bit. The same goes for you. We arrive fresh, and sometimes we get crumpled, but our value is fixed and permanent.

You deserve to be here. And you're allowed to be, do, and have everything that you wish for. You're perfectly enough, just as you are. Not when you are fifteen pounds lighter, earning $100K a year, married to "the one." Right now, exactly as you are, it is your birthright to be loved. You do not have to earn it. And let me tell you — nothing will make you more frustrated and exhausted than chasing something that you *already are*. Yep. Please read the sentence below slowly and out loud if you're willing, my friend (it's a text my tapping coach, Greg, sent me a while back that I've saved and look at often):

"Nothing will wear me out more quickly or more thoroughly than running around trying to be something that I already am."

Even if you drank too much last night, made a huge mistake at work, had awful parents you can't forgive yet, hurt a friend, got cheated on (or cheated yourself), feel behind at life, or made any of the other millions of mistakes we make that we allow to block the well-being and abundance that *is our birthright*.

No flaws, errors, or perceived faults change your deep, complete, and utter value as a human being. If you were lost on a mountain in a blizzard or disappeared on a hike, would a rescue team ask, before looking for you, "Who is this person?

Is she important and therefore worth the effort of a rescue? Is she verified on Instagram?" Of course not! They'd just look for you until you were found. Because your life *just as it is* makes you a VIP. And nothing you can do (or not do) can change that fact! *Nothing.*

Living a life of self-approval is remembering who you really are. It's knowing that the same power that brought everything into the physical world also brought you here at this particular time in history. Your contribution here matters. And a million "likes" won't make your life any more or less valuable — or more or less temporary. The approval of others is actually of *zero consequence* to you. When the Dalai Lama received the Nobel Peace Prize and was asked how he felt about it in an interview he said, "I am happy…" Then he followed up with, "…for the people who wanted me to win the Nobel Prize." Winning a Nobel Prize is one of the biggest accolades on the planet, right? Yep, but that wise soul knows something: external validation, however prestigious, isn't the thing. Can you imagine feeling even a *smidge* more this way? It would transform your entire world!

Overcoming Shyness

Speaking of a smidge of improvement, one thing I coach a lot on is overcoming shyness, even in small ways. It's easy to think that being shy and being an introvert are the same thing, but they're not. Introversion is the preference for quieter environments and time to restore oneself, alone. Shyness, on the other hand, can largely be the fear of criticism and of putting oneself out there and on the line.

You can absolutely reduce your shyness and get more from social interactions if that's a goal you have. Big groups naturally bring out the nerves for many (and can be very hard for people with anxiety). However, these situations are worth exploring.

Shyness can be a mask, a means of rejecting people before they have the opportunity to reject you. Here are some suggestions for lessening its hold on you:

1. Stop referring to yourself as shy. Words have power, and this self-identification disempowers you. Don't advertise your shyness, and it will instantly be less apparent to others.

2. Remember that most people feel tense or a little unsure of themselves in unfamiliar situations (you're in great company, even though your ego would have you believe that you're the only one who struggles). This doesn't make you shy; it makes you human.

3. Be a generous conversationalist by asking questions like, "How was your summer?" or "Do you live around here?" Open up a light and easy dialogue. Remember that other people are often shy, too, and you may be helping them by engaging them. Ever thought of that? *Giving wins!* Helping others open up is a generous act.

4. Lose the pressure to be perfect. In any social situation, good enough is just being polite!

5. Understand that visibility is not vulnerability. Taking the risk of being overlooked is far worse than missing out on what could be yours. You can even *force* yourself to be visible. When I was in my twenties, I was scared to speak up in corporate meetings with my superiors. So I forced myself to make a comment or ask a question within the first eight minutes of every single meeting. I timed it! Succeeding in almost anything requires being seen. I know that it helped my career. Shyness costs more than a little courage does.

DIRECT MESSAGE

Reducing shyness just means you get a little more comfortable being yourself in front of others. It means you open yourself up to more. It means more fun. What you do or do not decide to participate in is your call. Just don't confuse shyness with your fear.

Internal Validation

Feeling less attached to how people respond to me has made me far freer when it comes to business. I have an assistant, Kelly, who reads my emails, screens out the junk, and only forwards me the relevant stuff. This *used to* include some kind messages and praise. They would make me smile! But I've asked her not to send me those, either (the same way I don't see any of the hate emails I receive quite regularly). Because I don't want to do my work for praise. I want what I create to be determined by what I, not other people, "like." I want it to come from my intuitive leanings. Which, if you ask Kelly, ironically seems to boost the positive responses. The inner you knows what to do better than anyone!

One of the best lessons I've learned is not to make my internal vibe purely dependent on external circumstances. If something can't go your way, and you can still feel good and sure of yourself because you remember who the real you is, you're undefeatable. The most courageous people I observe are those who don't let what's going on in the outside world constantly dictate how they feel inside.

And just as you can screen out feedback, you can also screen out the stuff from your story that doesn't serve you well. I have a fantasy about what my TED Talk will be one day, and I think it will be something like this:

A Story of Two Girls

One grew up in shelters, surrounded by addiction, abuse, and chaos. Suffering was her almost daily experience.

The other had educated parents, did well at school, and felt sure of her parents' love for her.

They're...both me. So which story do I tell — especially to myself? The one that feels good! They're both true. And what you're not changing, even in your own mind, you're choosing. *That's how powerful your brain is.* It can change your personal story in any moment. Our mind can be our friend or our enemy.

We've all heard the traditional, superficial confidence advice that gets thrown around: "Fake it till you make it." I believe more in what Amy Cuddy shares in her record-breaking TED Talk on body language: "Fake it till you *become* it."

Think about it. If your dream is to run a marathon, and you actually do it, *what are you?* A marathon runner!

There's nothing fake about it. Or you.

And you're not a fake in the beginning stages of anything, either. You're what every established person once was: a beginner. And if you're able to be self-approving and humble enough to *be* a beginner, despite feeling self-conscious, look out, world! I read my old articles online sometimes, and I *cringe*. I was such a cheesy, anxious writer when I began. But...*so what?*

They got me started. And I needed those articles, exactly as they happened, in order to get better.

And on what bizarre planet are you supposed to know everything? Especially at the start of something new? Why would you ever expect that from yourself? There's a time for everything in your life. Learning. Pain. Struggle. Motion. Mastery. Rest. Can you welcome all stages and not be so serious about the less glamorous ones? Coach and author Tony Robbins said, "People are rewarded in public for what they practice for years in private." He's right. Everyone is struggling behind the scenes at something.

Because you're the only thinker in your universe, you get to choose how you interpret your life. So yes, *it actually is all about you*. Who or what else could it be about? Because reality is always your interpretation of it. Do you want a reactive life, where whatever other people say and do determines how you feel each day? Or would you prefer a self-directed, self-approving life where you get to pick how you respond to the world around you? You're going to die no matter which way you decide. So why not make a choice that's a little more... extraordinary? Fun? Powerful? Inspiring to those around you?

There is no end, just the present moment. Ever notice that? It's always just the next moment. It's all there'll ever be while you're still breathing. I know that undergoing a major perspective change can be really daunting. The goal that we're setting here doesn't have to be "never needing external approval ever again, from this moment forward." That would be impossible. But you can take a step in that direction. Ask yourself: *Can I realize that I'm doing okay? Can I like myself a little more — just for today? Can I lighten up and enjoy myself a little more, right this second?*

DIRECT MESSAGE

Your entire life is series of "right-this-second" moments. That's all you'll ever experience: the present moment you're in right now. The only finish line is the grave. Manage the present second well, and we're all good here!

So what's your mood like, in this specific moment? At a seminar I attended a while back, an extremely successful entrepreneur said (to applause!), "Hey, we are *all* learning as we go. I make mistakes and cringe all the time at them! That's why I keep winning — mistakes don't stop this tushie hustlin'!" That's probably why we all showed up. She didn't take herself so seriously, even in front of a big crowd that could've scared her. And when you can be easier about the present moment, an enhanced mood naturally follows. And people want to be around you.

Day to day, when life goes wrong, you can also do things to help yourself remain light. You can scatter positive affirmations on Post-its around your home. My faves say, "You sexy thang, you!" and "Joy is my natural state." You can set alarms on your phone with upbeat reminders that can go off at random times of the day. I have one that says, "Everything is working out perfectly." You can make all your passwords an uplifting affirmation that you'll type over and over again. Like: lifeisgood. (I'd call that pretty fly for a WiFi.)

Because life *is* good.

No matter where you are right now, look what you've

survived! You've made it here! Salute yourself. I know it hasn't been easy. But you're okay. And you will continue to be okay.

No one else can ever give you your power. *It has to be claimed by you.* Will you take its open hand and walk along with it a while? And as a result of the more powerful, self-approving you, show the world what you got? Because living with less need for approval will give you a dangerous level of personal freedom. Just visualize what you will do with all that free rein! The alternative is powerlessly waiting your whole life for your dreams to come to you.

When I was in Bali, sitting in a guided meditation, an answer came to me about why we're all here. People question their purpose a lot and struggle to identify passions. But my higher self told me, "Just fix what makes you sad."

Simple, right? The wisest things always are. Understand what hurts your heart most in this world and make it better, no matter how small the corner of the world you touch is.

For me, the saddest thing is a human being who lives a puny life because they're so busy checking their metaphorical likes. Put your phone down for a second and look around you. See how good your life really is. Think of all the sheer possibilities before you! The world is starving for more from you. The real you. Those gifts you were born with that might be hiding right now? They exist to be used! Sometimes we just forget what's real because we're so distracted by the *illusion* of approval that we stay hidden and safe. I heard once that development and growth are like an egg. If an egg's broken by outside force, life ends. If it's broken by inside force, life begins. Great things begin from inside. What's waiting to come out from inside you? Only you know. It starts by accepting your own friend request.

Following others or being part of a group of people who inspire you is wonderful if it helps keep you focused on your unique desires. Following a crowd because it's easy or because that's what everyone else is doing can work for a while, yes. But just be careful not to miss your exit, like I did when I got swept up in that imaginary race in Central Park.

Now, can we go have some fun?

The end.

...Or is it the beginning?

Because You Always Deserve More Good Things!

Here's some accessory advice to elevate your life on the daily. Consider it your quick cheat sheet for more everyday approval-free living magic.

Smile when someone make a negative comment about your boss outfit (or makes any stupid remark). And respond to a compliment with grace.

When someone snarks, do not defend yourself, ever. In your lack of defensiveness, you are always safe. When we get defensive and sensitive, bad stuff can happen. So smile. And when it comes to taking a compliment, say thank you! That's all. It's a gift, so appreciate it. Don't make the person giving you the gift have to defend it.

"Gorgeous dress."

"Thank you!"

Not "Oh, it has a hole in it and it's too tight — I bought it ten pounds ago." A simple thank-you is gracious and swift and more likely to put you on the receiving end of many more word gifts.

Don't talk about your health.

There's an old English saying, "Do not tell others about your indigestion. 'How are you?' is a greeting, not a question."

Health is a boring topic. Those of us who don't talk about our health tend to be the healthiest of all.

Know that love is what makes a family. And there are ways to discuss your actual family if they're weird and talking about them makes you uncomfortable.

Loyal friends count as family, and you can tell them that!

I used to be uncomfy talking about my dead dad and my spread-out family. So I'd keep it short! "I lost my dad when I was young. My mom lives in the UK." That's it! Then ask questions of the person you're talking to. It'll get you out of sharing any details you want to avoid and make you an engaging conversationalist, too.

Add, don't subtract.

We live in an inclusive universe. What we focus on expands. So if you want to subtract something — a negative pal, too much wine, a shitty job — focus on what you can add in its place, such as an uplifting pal, a running group (or other healthy habit), some LinkedIn updates and reach-outs to open your career network.

Stop unconscious self-sabotage!

Are you sabotaging something just because it's familiar — a relationship, a good career, a friendship? Sabotage is just short-term relief at the cost of longer-term gain. Think: What do you really want? And are your actions aligning?

Know that everything is good for something.

When I was a kid I saw my dad pick up a pink pill from the floor and swallow it. "What was that?" I asked, shocked.

"I dunno," he answered. "But it's good for something!"

Admittedly, this is a dreadful example of a reasonable truth. Even the stuff that can or does harm you, such as a breakup, a health scare, or a fight with someone you love, can have some positive effects if you let it. What's the good? It's in there somewhere.

Reframe the inconvenient.

Do you feel annoyed when your spouse works late? Hey, her passion for her work attracted you to her in the first place, right? How can you see the situation differently?

Be the irresistible friend in your group.

If you wanna be a friend magnet, these qualities won't fail you:

1. Optimism
2. Being easy to be with
3. Taking the initiative by making fun, specific plans. Not "Wanna hang out soon?" but "Wanna try the new vegan restaurant in Brooklyn with me this Friday night at 7:00?"

Leave the (metaphorical) party sooner than you "should."

No one ever said, "I wish I'd stayed in that cruddy job six months longer." As the old saying goes, familiarity breeds incumbency. When something starts to feel bad — a job, a relationship, anything — and stays bad for longer than two to three months, remember to trust your happiness!

Make your affirmation really work this time.

Be relaxed when you say it. When you're uptight, you don't let the magic in.

Impress a job interviewer to no end.

Use the *precise* words in the job description. Does she want a driven, team-playing self-starter? Great! Use those exact words to describe yourself (if they're true). Don't try to be a hero by being original. Make it easy for her to say yes – you've arrived! *Cue confetti drop.*

Make beautiful things part of your day.

Take a walk and look up at the sky. Put your palm on a tree for thirty seconds. Pet your cat. Experience daily beauty on purpose.

Give everyone the benefit of the doubt.

Trust me. Your life will be a million times happier this way. If you *think* somebody has wronged you, ask them, don't accuse them.

Recover from a mistake, fast.

Mistakes are actually much less risky than we make them out to be. Hitting Reply All by accident or having an uncomfortable confrontation that you regret can often be fixed with a swift honest talk and/or an apology. Or even nothing at all (it's possible you're exaggerating the size of your mistake).

Make small talk like a boss.

The best way to engage another person is by asking questions, especially those that can't be answered with a yes or no response.

Questions like, "How did you two meet?" "How do you know Sally?" and "What are you doing this summer?" all open up easy, light dialogue.

With a little time and some back-and-forth, the common ground will appear: "We met online also, funny story…," "Sally and I worked together, too…" "Oh, I love Florida."

Remember that happiness is a decision you make, not an emotion you feel.

And the only decider in your life is you.

Live like a boss.

Stop checking your likes. And doing anything else that slows you down.

Master the Pay-Raise Script

My Time-Tested, Industry-Tested Approach to Asking for a Pay Raise, a.k.a. My "You've Got This!" Script

The Opening

Begin with the "we are in this together" approach:

I want to let you know that I love it here, [manager name]. I have truly enjoyed the past X months and feel really pleased with my contribution to the team. If we can, I would like to discuss my current salary. Is this a conversation that we can have today?

I am so grateful for this company. You have taught me so much, and I really like X and Y [you can mention team members, systems, projects].

I feel there is so much more growth possible for me

here, and I am excited about what more I can bring to my role and how much more I can contribute in the coming months.

I want you to know that I am committed to our team and do not want to be in a position where I feel open to any outside roles.

The only thing that could make an external conversation possible would be the compensation offered.

Then be silent.

You might be asked if you have been looking. If you have, you can say:

Yes, but I have not engaged in any real conversation, and I would prefer not to.

If you have not, you can say:

I have not been looking.

Then move on to the Ask.

The Ask

Now we get to the juicy part:

My industry friends [and/or research] have told me people in my role typically make around X percent more.

Give your boss a moment to absorb this. Trust me, it is extremely unlikely that they have not been presented with this argument before.

Typically, they ask for a number (or more information), to which you can respond:

> Currently I am making $X. My understanding is that market rate for my position is $X, and I would like to match that, if possible.

Then say nothing. Do not overspeak.

The Close

This is the time to be extra appreciative of and thankful to your boss. I like to say:

> Thank you so much for listening. I am happy we had this conversation. I look forward to our next discussion and then working with you to achieve our goals over the next six to twelve months.

Your patience and gratitude matter throughout this process!

Possible Outcomes

There are pretty much just three possible outcomes:

1. Manager says yes, and you get exactly what you want.
2. Manager says no because there is no money budgeted, so you ask for other perks instead.
3. Manager says no to the raise and asks you to improve your performance.

If you get outcome #1, rock on! If not, here's how to manage the other two.

No Budget — Ask for Additional Perks

Perks you can ask for in lieu of a raise:

- Additional vacation days
- Permission to work remotely (decide ahead of time how often you'd like to work remotely, and specify it in your request)
- Additional team support or exposure to new projects you might have an interest in

Remember, you can request to review your salary again within a certain time frame and get a commitment from your boss as to when you will discuss it again (and you can ask for permission to mark this "check-in" in both of your calendars).

So often, we think it's just a salary increase that's the goal, when many other options are available that can boost our joy at work, too. Some of the other perks that there is often untapped budget for include:

- A work-related course
- Educational assistance for any studies you are doing
- Permission to attend conferences or other events that interest you

Sample Conversation

Manager: Sarah, we would love to give you what you are asking for, but it's not in the budget for this year. We can revisit this within X months from now.

Employee: Thanks for letting me know, Amy. I really appreciate you looking into it for me. I have a couple of other questions, if that is okay?

M: Please go ahead.

E: If there is no room to move on my salary, may I request one or two other things in the interim that would be really helpful to me?

M: You can certainly ask, yes.

E: My friends in this industry have work-from-home flexibility on Fridays — is this something we can discuss?

M: It could be. Are you talking about every week?

E: Yes.

M: Okay, I will get back to you on that. Is there a second thing?

E: Yes, I'm really interested in attending more events and conferences in our industry. There are a few coming up that I would love to go to. Is there a budget for these?

Regardless of what the manager says, here's a positive, professional way to wrap it up:

E: Thanks again for listening, Amy. I look forward to hearing from you on these. I will also mark my calendar for the date you set to revisit our initial chat. If you need anything else from me or have any questions for me, please ask. I really appreciate everything you are doing for me.

Higher Performance Required First

In some cases, your manager will want you to take on more responsibilities and/or will want to see an improvement in your overall work performance. This is okay — it's a common outcome! Here is a good way to handle that situation.

Sample Conversation

Manager: In order for us to give you what you are asking for, we need you to be performing at a higher level. Let me explain what that is....

Employee: Thanks for explaining this to me, Amy. I am excited to take this direction and create a game plan with you to get where I need to be. I am confident I can get to the level you need me to be within X months. To clarify, once I get there and fulfill what is expected of me, will I be in a position to receive the increase that I am hoping for? And if so, can you and I please have perhaps biweekly check-ins to ensure that I am on track?

M: Yes, that is the goal.

E: Thanks again for listening, Amy. I look forward to working on all these objectives, and I will send you an invite for our regular check-ins to ensure that I am on track. If you need anything additional from me, please let me know. I really appreciate your time and help.

Remember this — asking matters! This bears repeating. If you don't ask, the answer is always no.

- It's about *more* than money.
- Timing, performance, and confidence must be peak.
- Conduct your own research!
- An optimistic approach matters.
- Negotiation works — listen first.
- Convey enthusiasm for your work, and when ready, just ask!

DIRECT MESSAGE (OVER AND OUT!)

Remember what Timothy Ferriss said: "A person's success in life can usually be measured by the number of uncomfortable conversations he or she is willing to have."

Check this:

❑   Start research immediately!
❑   Download my confidence workbook, available at Susie-Moore.com.
❑   Speak to two or three recruiters.
❑   Conduct industry research with peers (two or three people).
❑   Gather feedback and support from coworkers and industry friends.
❑   Review the above scripts as a guide for preparation.
❑   When the timing is right, *ask*!

Still feeling scared? Remember that photo of yourself as a kid we talked about earlier? Do it for her. She's relying on you.

Then: Celebrate! No matter what, you did it. That's enough. Brava!

Acknowledgments

I'd like to thank my husband, Heath, for being my biggest supporter and partner in everything. I've never met such a secure, supportive, awesome human.

So much appreciation to my four sisters, Natasza, Nikki, Nancy, and Liz, for giving me a great example of grace, strength, and doing life your way.

To my mom, Jasia, for reading this book with me, adding color to my memories, and for being such a uniquely strong, wise woman who doesn't take life too seriously.

Wendy and Peter Collins, I'm beyond honored and blessed to call you my family. Thank you for giving me the best gift of my life.

Jess Novak, I couldn't have made this book without your help. Thank you for your incredible smarts, generosity, and insight.

Laura Noonan, thank you for being such a reliable, wonderful friend and workmate (we can't get by without you).

Farnoosh Torabi, you're my fifth sister!

Alexis Cappie-Wood, you've been my best friend for nearly twenty years. I owe you more than you'll ever understand!

Derek Flanzraich and the entire Greatist team, thanks for giving me an incredible platform and allowing me to share my stories.

To my brilliant friends Adam Auriemma, Laura Belgray, Ruth Soukup, Melyssa Griffin, Libby Kane, Fiona McKinnon, Kim Hollis, Luisa Zhou, Jamie Jensen, Elizabeth Rider, Julie Solomon, Bruce Littlefield, Scott Stewart, Cami Galles…you are beyond loved.

Michele Martin, thank you for believing in me. And for your no-nonsense, honest approach. I absolutely love it!

Georgia Hughes and the New World Library team, I'm honored to be part of your squad. Thanks for welcoming me with such enthusiasm!

Thanks go to every inspiring and brave author out there. I'd list them all, but this book would never end. So for brevity's sake I'd love to share special appreciation for Wayne Dyer, Robin Sharma, Byron Katie, Shakti Gawain, Eckhart Tolle, Shawn Achor, Ainslie MacLeod, Deepak Chopra, James Altucher, Jessica Knoll, Elizabeth Gilbert, Steven Pressfield, Amy Cuddy, James Allen, Michael Hyatt, Farnoosh Torabi, Jack Canfield, Abraham-Hicks, Dale Carnegie, Don Miguel Ruiz, Viktor Frankl, and of course David J. Schwarz.

Notes

Introduction

p. 5   *"One of the saddest things in life"*: Robin Sharma, quoted in Maxine Topping, *U Owe You* (Parker, CO: Outskirts Press, 2018), 105.

Chapter 1: Your Parents Effed You Up

p. 17   *I found* The Magic of Thinking Big: David J. Schwartz, *The Magic of Thinking Big* (1959; repr., New York: Fireside, 1987).

Chapter 2: No One Else Knows What They're Doing, Either

p. 30   *"For all sad words of tongue and pen"*: These lines come from John Greenleaf Whittier's 1856 poem "Maud Muller."

p. 37   *"As within, so without"*: Eckhart Tolle, *The Power of Now: A Guide to Spiritual Enlightenment* (Novato, CA: New World Library, 1999), 79.

Chapter 3: How to Always End Up on Top

p. 41   *antidepressants are prescribed at least four times more:* Lea Winerman, "By the Numbers: Antidepressant Use on the Rise," *Monitor on Psychology* 48, no. 10 (November 2017), 120, https://www.apa.org/monitor/2017/11/numbers.

p. 50   *"If we all threw our problems"*: Regina Brett, *God Never Blinks: 50 Lessons for God's Little Detours* (New York: Grand Central Publishing, 2010), lesson 40.

Chapter 4: So What?

p. 68   *"It is a great insult to the collective intelligence"*: James Snell, "The Dalai Lama Deserves Criticism, Not Adulation," *Huffington Post*, November 11, 2013, https://www.huffingtonpost .co.uk/james-snell/dalai-lama-criticism_b_4421553.html.

p. 72   *"You think that love has to last forever"*: Joey Comeau, *Overqualified* (Toronto: ECW Press, 2009), 61.

p. 73   *So one day he gave up socks*: Len Fisher, "Why Einstein Didn't Wear Socks and the Nature of Scientific Inquiry," May 11, 2016, edited extract of a talk delivered on *Ockhams's Razor*, an ABC podcast, https://www.abc.net.au/radionational/programs /ockhamsrazor/einstein-socks-nature-scientific-inquiry /7395862.

Chapter 5: Love Yourself, Especially When You Don't "Deserve" It

p. 79   *"You have been criticizing yourself for years"*: Louise Hay, *You Can Heal Your Life* (1984; repr., Carlsbad, CA: Hay House, 2004), 9.

Chapter 6: It's Okay If People Don't Like You

p. 95   *A snakebite can kill you, right? Wrong!*: Dr. Wayne W. Dyer, Facebook post, January 17, 2012, https://www.facebook.com /drwaynedyer/posts/resentment-is-like-venom-that-continues -to-pour-through-your-system-doing-its-po/10150533926051030/.

Chapter 7: See the World through
Comedy-Colored Glasses

p. 113   *"One of the things that I think we should all do"*: Alain de Botton, "Alain de Botton on Pessimism," School of Life Sunday Sermons, YouTube video, 24:22, February 4, 2013, https://www.youtube.com/watch?v=Aw10LtuJOXQ.

p. 116   *"Success orbits around happiness"*: Shawn Achor, *The Happiness Advantage: How a Positive Brain Fuels Success in Work and Life* (New York: Crown, 2010), 38.

p. 118   *"Here's a great spiritual practice for you"*: Eckhart Tolle (@EckhartTolle), Twitter, April 15, 2018, 8:37 PM, https://twitter.com/eckharttolle/status/985678634504499200?lang=en.

p. 125   *"Thirty-five years may not seem long"*: Jason Duaine Hahn, "Woman, 35, Who Died of Cancer Writes Her Own Obituary: Life 'Was Good!,'" *People*, April 18, 2019, https://people.com/human-interest/bailey-jean-matheson-writes-own-obituary.

Chapter 8: Second Opinions Aren't Better
Than Your First Feeling

p. 128   *"I wish I'd had the courage to live"*: Bronnie Ware, *The Top Five Regrets of the Dying: A Life Transformed by the Dearly Departing* (London: Hay House, 2011), 37.

p. 133   *"When you spend time alone"*: Susie Moore, "What Sara Blakely Wished She Knew in Her 20s," *Marie Claire*, November 4, 2014, https://www.marieclaire.com/politics/news/a11508/sara-blakely-interview.

Chapter 9: Ask, "What's Missing?"

p. 144   *"In many shamanic societies"*: Gabrielle Roth, *Maps to Ecstasy: The Healing Power of Movement* (Novato, CA: New World Library, 1998), xv.

p. 152   *"Be brave enough to be bad"*: Jon Acuff, Facebook, October 3, 2018, https://www.facebook.com/authorjonacuff/posts/be -brave-enough-to-be-bad-at-something-new/1015103860001 4950.

Chapter 10: Great News: It's Your Fault

p. 164   *"You are doomed to make choices"*: Wayne Dyer, *I Can See Clearly Now* (Carlsbad, CA: Hay House, 2014), 360.

p. 177   *"Antifragility is beyond resilience"*: Nassim Nicholas Taleb, *Antifragile: Things That Gain from Disorder* (New York: Random House, 2014), 3.

Chapter 11: Fall Madly in Love with Rejection

p. 188   *Dan Baker breaks this down brilliantly*: Dan Baker, *What Happy People Know: How the New Science of Happiness Can Change Your Life for the Better* (New York: Rodale, 2003).

Chapter 12: Ask

p. 198   *"Don't make assumptions"*: Don Miguel Ruiz, *The Four Agreements: A Practical Guide to Personal Freedom* (San Rafael, CA: Amber-Allen, 1997), 1.

p. 199   *"A person's success in life can usually be measured"*: Timothy Ferriss, *The 4-Hour Workweek*, revised edition (New York: Crown, 2009), 47.

p. 200   *"Success isn't passive"*: Elizabeth Gilbert, "Quote of the Day: Manifesting Your Blessings with Elizabeth Gilbert," Write in Color, https://www.writeincolor.com/2011/10/28/quote-of-the -day-manifesting-your-blessings-by-elizabeth-gilbert.

p. 200   *"a woman who routinely negotiates her salary"*: Linda Babcock and Sara Laschever, *Women Don't Ask: The High Cost of Avoiding Negotiation — and Positive Strategies for Change* (2003; repr., New York: Bantam, 2007), 7.

p. 203   *"Every relationship is one of give and take"*: Deepak Chopra,
          *The Seven Spiritual Laws of Success: A Practical Guide to the
          Fulfillment of Your Dreams* (San Rafael, CA: Amber-Allen,
          1994), 29.

Chapter 13: Let It Be Easy

p. 210   *"There is no stress in this world"*: Wayne W. Dyer, Facebook,
          April 30, 2012, https://www.facebook.com/drwaynedyer/posts
          /there-is-no-stress-in-the-world-only-people-thinking
          -stressful-thoughts/10150782022891030.
p. 213   *"Adversities, no matter what they are"*: Shawn Achor, *The
          Happiness Advantage* (New York: Crown, 2010), 126.

Chapter 14: You're Going to Be Okay

p. 231   *"Fake it till you become it"*: Amy Cuddy, "Your Body Language
          May Shape Who You Are," TED Talk, June 2012, https://www
          .ted.com/talks/amy_cuddy_your_body_language_shapes_who
          _you_are.

About the Author

Susie Moore is a former Silicon Valley sales director turned life coach and advice columnist. Her work been featured on the *Today* show and on *Oprah*, as well as in *Business Insider*, the *Huffington Post*, *Forbes*, *MONEY*, and *Marie Claire*, and she's the resident life coach columnist for *Greatist*. Susie's work and insights have been shared by celebrities and thought leaders, including Arianna Huffington, Paulo Coelho, Kris Jenner, and Sara Blakely. Her first book, *What If It Does Work Out?*, was named by *Entrepreneur* as a "Business Book Entrepreneurs Must Read to Dominate Their Industry." Formerly based in New York City, she currently lives in Miami with her husband, Heath, and their Yorkshire terrier, Coconut.